# FROGLEY,
# COCKHEAD & CRUTCH

# FROGLEY,
# COCKHEAD & CRUTCH

## A Celebration of Humorous Names
## from Oxfordshire's History

### Paul Sullivan

First published 2015

The History Press
The Mill, Brimscombe Port
Stroud, Gloucestershire, GL5 2QG
www.thehistorypress.co.uk

British Library Cataloguing in Publication Data.
A catalogue record for this book is available from the British Library.

ISBN 978 0 7509 6300 8

Typesetting and origination by The History Press
Printed in Great Britain

CONTENTS

*In memory of my very best friend,*

*Ian Randal Howgego*

*1961–1997*

# Contents

# Introduction: Name Calling

| | |
|---|---|
| **Florence Frogley** | 1857–1923, Headington |
| **Willy Cockhead** | 1790–1871, Witney |
| **Cornelius Crutch** | 1832–1864, Wootton-by-Woodstock |

The journey from birth to birth certificate is a surprisingly hazardous one. If you have a funny surname, for example, it is important to choose accompanying names carefully. The fact that this hazard isn't always heeded – or perhaps it is being gleefully embraced – can be witnessed by the presence of Rhoda Turtle, Annie May Kill, Tommy Rumble and a hundred others in the following pages.

If there's nothing funny about your surname per se, you can still raise a giggle or two by prefixing it with amusing or wilfully obscure forenames. Step forward Christ-Gift New, Ivor Brain and Urina Hedges – all featured in this naming and shaming volume.

Occasionally the humour in the name is a cruel whim of time. The family of Adolph Perish was perfectly happy with his name until a more famous Adolf appeared on the political stage. All those pre-'70s Wallies, such as Wally Tulip of Banbury and Willy Wally Wheeler of Woodstock, had no idea that they would one day be synonymous with foolishness. And what a cruel fate befell the huge army of Fannys – they have a dedicated entry in this book – when their name was hijacked twice in quick succession! (The use of the word 'fanny' to denote a certain part of the female anatomy is first recorded in print in England in 1879 after several years in oral usage. Over the pond, the word's alternative meaning as the human derriere cropped up on the printed page in 1928 and has been at the bottom of the class ever since.)

A person's life can be mapped as a journey through the oddities of personal nomenclature. Back in my childhood, when a classroom was far less likely to be filled with such twenty-first-century names as Ferrari Porsche, Unique Keanu, Huckleberry Banjo and Dylan Oxford United (all real), there were still some glorious oddities. My best friend through school and university was the sorely missed Ian Randal Howgego, who left the story far too early at the tender age of 35. I have also shared classrooms with members of the Blood, Death and Onions families – the latter two trying to hide the truth behind an apostrophe, in the form of De'ath and O'Nions. There were Eastcrabs, Lillycraps, Boggis' and Scattergoods. The contrasting landscapes of Heather Moor and Heather Marsh shared a desk, university-era pals Lisa Simpson, Tom Cobbley and Steven Fry all discovered unwelcome links with famous namesakes, and the unfortunate parental blindspots of Dick Blow and Pat Mycock just had to grin and bear it.

Some of the imaginatively monickered people in this book lived out their lives in Berkshire – Abingdon, Didcot, Drayton, Faringdon, Radley, Wallingford, Wantage and Wytham only made the leap into Oxfordshire in 1974. It works the other way too – Caversham was part of Oxfordshire until 1911, when it succumbed to the gravitational pull of Reading in Berkshire.

Ploughley and Bullingdon, meanwhile, have disappeared. Ploughley was an administrative unit known as a 'hundred', a large rural district centring on (but not including) Bicester. It gained a new lease of life as one of Oxfordshire's seven Rural Districts, but was abolished in 1974. The region defined by Ploughley is now part of the Cherwell district. Bullingdon hundred was swallowed by Ploughley in the mid-nineteenth century. It encompassed an area including Nuneham Courtenay in the south, Beckley in the north, Waterperry in the east and Marston in the west. All of which adds nicely to the general name-calling and confusion.

*Frogley, Cockhead & Crutch* is a celebration of ordinary people (and places) with extraordinary names. It acts as a dire warning from history – or an unfortunate nudge of encouragement – for future generations in the county of Oxfordshire.

*Paul Sullivan, 2015*

# 1
# CRAZY NAMES

Some people think it's crazy to have children. Some parents agree, and express their feelings in the names of their beloved offspring.

| | |
|---|---|
| **ARAMINTA BATTY** | 1845–1927, Henley |
| **MADGITTA BATTY** | Born 1879, Henley |
| **EDWIN BERK** | Born 1826, Oxford |
| **ED CASE** | Born 1858, Witney |
| **CECIL T. DAFT** | Born 1917, Headington |
| **FRANK DUNCE** | Born 1879, Witney |
| **MARY FOOL** | 1898–1911, Caversham |
| **ARTHUR MORRIS FREAKY** | Married 1884, Oxford |
| **MAD HAYNES** | Born 1902, Banbury |
| **PSYCHE HOUGHTON** | Born Oxford, 1879 |

**WALLY WILLY HOWLING**                    1905–1994, Abingdon

**LIZZIE LOONEY**                          Born 1884, Headington

**BATTY LORGE**                            Born 1801, Burford

**FRED FANNIS C. NUTT**                    Born 1891, Oxford

**CHARLIE NUTTER**                 Born 1804, Neithrop, Banbury

**MARY ANN NUTTY**                         Died Oxford, 1850

**ALF PRATT PRATT**                Born 1908, Chipping Norton

**MARMADUKE ROLAND PRATT**                 Born 1828, Oxford

Marmaduke Roland Pratt was father of Marmaduke Roland Pratt
(1851–1915) and grandfather of … yes, you guessed it … Marmaduke
Roland Pratt (1881–1935). The second of these Marmaduke Pratts,
a grocer, was chief witness in the trial of Marian Louise Grainger
at the Oxford Assizes in 1877. Grainger was accused of murder-
ing her husband James by drunkenly wounding him by stabbing
him in the left buttock with a stiletto, or a knife, or by throwing a
tumbler at him. No one seemed quite sure which. Marian claimed
her drunken husband had accidentally stabbed himself with a knife
during a quarrel. Whatever happened, the wound festered and the
man died. Marmaduke Pratt, the couple's son-in-law, explained how
Marian had asked him to visit during James' decline, asking him if
he thought her husband would die. 'I have no doubt about it,' said
Pratt, to which Marian responded, 'Good God, whatever shall I do?
God only knows how I shall ever get over it. How could I have
done such a thing? But I never did it!' In summing up, the judge
commented that Pratt clearly 'had no very kindly feelings towards
his mother-in-law'. Squinting through the drunken haze, the jury
delivered a verdict of not guilty. (*Jackson's Oxford Journal*, Saturday,
7 July 1877)

| | |
|---|---|
| **MARY JOHN PRATT** | 1842–1907, Headington |
| **WILLIAM RAVE** | Born 1856, Chipping Norton |
| **FANNY RAVES** | Born 1883, Henley |
| **SARAH ANN SANE** | Born 1851, Enstone |
| **CHARLIE SILLY** | Born 1875, Headington |
| **MARY MANIA STEPHENS** | Married 1860, Witney |
| **DICK THICK** | Married in Headington in 1888, and died a year later |
| **SILLY WATERS** | Born 1898, Bloxham |

**2**

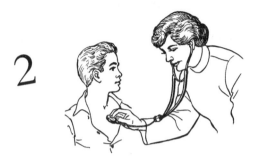

# Doctor, Doctor ... !

All manner of ailments and medical symptoms await us
in the pages of Oxfordshire's surgery of surnames.

| | |
|---|---|
| Hugh Agscough | 1818–1879, Witney |
| Rehab Allwright | Born 1843, Cholsey |
| Lizzie Blister | Born 1842, Oxford |
| Henry Boils | Died 1846, Thame |
| George Coff | Born 1828, Oxford |
| Dicky Hart | 1813–1885, Wantage |
| Elizabeth Headache | Died 1854, Bicester |
| Daniel P. Health | Born 1891, Kingham |
| Massey Leper Laper | At Oriel College, Oxford, in the 1841 census, age 20 |

# ETHEL M. PAIN
Born 1892, Wantage

# MOSES PATIENT
Born 1649, Cote

# CONSTANCE PAYNE
Born 1885, Headington

# GEORGE SEPTIMUS PAYNE
1851–1933, Banbury, Abingdon and Oxford

John Payne opened Payne & Son silversmiths and jewellers in Wallingford in 1790, with other branches later opening in Abingdon and Banbury. George Septimus Payne inherited the Abingdon shop in 1874, moving it to No. 131 High Street, Oxford in 1889. Formerly occupied by James Sheard, a watchmaker, the Oxford premises are surmounted by a lifesize, white Great Dane, holding a giant fob watch in its mouth, as a pun on 'watch dog'. The watch used to have painted hands; but these were painted over in the 1960s to put an end to the constant stream of people calling into the shop to report that the clock was telling the wrong time.

CHARLOTTE PILES      Born 1791, Swinbrook

FANNY PILL      Born 1858, Witney

ANN POX      Born 1839, Church Hanborough

DINOSIC PROSSER      Born 1796, Yarnton

EMILY KING RICKETTS      Born 1856, Abingdon

HUGH HAMILTON SICK      Born 1877, Radley

CAROLINE SNEEZUM      Born 1833, Rotherfield Greys

ANN STROKE      Born 1818, Henley

WILLY TUMER [SIC]      Born 1876, Pyrton, Henley

V. TYPHUS      Born 1832, Abingdon

WILLY WART      Born 1846, Culham

# 3 TOO LATE FOR THE DOCTOR ...

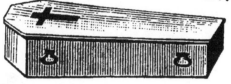

Sometimes the symptoms take their natural course,
and there is no hope for the following victims.

**ALFRED VICTOR CARCASS**     Died 1887, Banbury

**BENJAMIN COFFIN**     Born 1826, Oxford

**DAISY DEATH**     Born 1887, Oxford

**PHYLLIS GRAVE**     1858–1938, Rotherfield Greys

**PHIL GRAVES**     Born 1854, languishing in Oxford Gaol in 1885
Poor George Graves, aged 14, inmate of Abingdon Union Workhouse,
died on 3 February 1842. The cause of death was recorded as
'inflammation of the brain, and not from external injuries'.

**HARRY HEARSE**     Born 1897, Curbridge

**WILLIAM HUNG**     Born 1795, Wallingford

**TRISTRAM PINE-COFFIN**     Married 1915, Thame

# GUY STIFF
Born 1880, Oxford

# JOHN JAMES TOMBS TOMBS
Born 1846, Witney

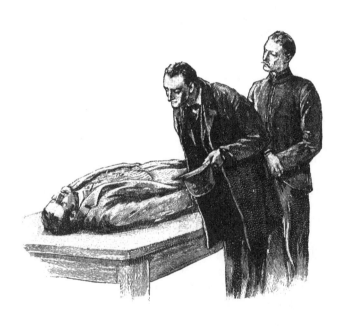

# 4

# IT'S ALL A STATE OF MIND

Many names paint a picture of the human condition –
how we're feeling, how we look upon the world around us,
how we're looked upon by others. Listed together,
they present an intriguing scene worthy of a Hogarth
print or, bringing the canvas forward a couple of
centuries, a comic strip in *The Beano* or *Viz*.

| | |
|---|---|
| **PARFITT FORD ALLRIGHT** | Born 1845, Eye and Dunsden |
| **PARFET ALLWRIGHT** | Born 1839, Cholsey |
| **STRANGE ANDREWS** | 1869–1941, Ploughley |
| **TEMPER ARISS** | Born 1817, Banbury |
| **EDWARD ARTHUR ATTACK** | Born in Romford, Essex, 1860; married 1888, Headington |
| **LOVELESS BARTHOLOMEW** | Born 1846, Caversham |
| **CAROLINA BLISS** | 1820–1889, Chipping Norton |

## CRISS BOILING
Born 1868, Thame

## JANE BOILING
Born 1860, Thame

On 12 November 1884, Jane Boiling took Thomas Oliver to court, claiming that he had both insulted and assaulted her. Oliver had found her in one of his houses, speaking with the tenant who lived there. There was bad blood between Boiling and Oliver, and he manhandled her off the premises. The assault charge could not be proved, however, and the case went off the boil.

## GEORGIANA BORE
Born 1833, Bletchingdon

## JOSHUA JONES COOL
Born 1837, Hook Norton

## JACK CRACKS
Born 1887, Bicester

## LIZZIE HAPPY DAWS
Born 1888, Oxford

## FRED DUDE
Born 1858, Henley

## MABEL SWEET EAGLES
Born 1883, Oxford

## HOPE EAST
Born 1845, Goring-on-Thames

## URINA M. GOODE
Born 1912, Banbury

## MERCY ING
Died 1857, Thame

## JESSIE GEORGE LOVELOCK WALLACE JOLLY
Born 1880, Oxford

## FREE LACEY
1872–1952, Ploughley

## EDDIE LAUGHTER
Married 1845, Woodstock

## GRACE LIFE
1892–1988, Oxford

## Henry Cheater Lines
Born 1852, Banbury

## Fanny Jolly Lingham
1829–1875, Headington

## Fail Macey
Born 1833, Caversfield

## Henry Tripp Mean
Born 1819, Henley

## Leah Batts Merry
Born 1860, Witney

## Hope More
Born 1830, Oxford

## Harmer C. Ogle
Born 1843, Oxford

*Ogling in St Giles*: The four statues that surmount the Taylorian Institute in Oxford (the section of the Ashmolean Museum facing on to St Giles) symbolise the literary heritage of France, Germany, Italy and Spain. Unofficially, they were said to have been modelled on four beautiful local girls called Ogle who lived on St Giles. The girls in question were sisters Janet (b.1821), Mary (b.1824), and twins Amelia and Caroline (b.1826). The Institute opened in 1845.

| | |
|---|---|
| EVIS CROSS PARGETER | Born 1867, Banbury |
| SALOME PEACHEY | Born 1870, Sarsden |
| COSMO POUNCEY | Born 1911, Headington |
| BOB PRIGG | Born 1874, Headington |
| HILDA LOVE QUELCH | 1893–1975, Bullingdon |
| HATE ROLY | Born 1899, Oxford |
| MERCY SAVAGE | 1788–1866, Woodstock |
| MAY STRIKE | Born 1811, Oxford |
| WINIFRED MAY WANT | 1914–2004, Witney |
| MERCY WEAVER | Married 1870, Banbury |
| LANCELOT WILD | Will dated 1752, Oxfordshire |
| OGLE WINTLE | Born 1834, Headington |
| ANGER MARRIE WOODWARD | Born 1900, Chadlington |
| ED WRONG | 1890–1928, Headington, |

# Show Us What You're Made Of!

Surnames can give interesting hints at an individual's
physical attributes or personal tendencies. Most of them
are misleading, we may assume – for example, although
Girlie Anson was, indeed, a girl, it is highly unlikely
that Tempest Slinger behaved like a Victorian Zeus.

**GIRLIE ESMAY ANSON**            1932–1994, Oxford

**LIZZIE CROOK ARIES**       Born 1873, Stoke Lyne, Bicester

**WILLY BARKASS**           Born 1801, Shirburn

**SHUTE BARRINGTON**   Of Beckett Hall in Shrivenham (1734–1826)
*Shute to win*: Shute Barrington was born at Beckett Hall in Shrivenham
and was an alumnus of Merton College, Oxford. He won a church
hat-trick, becoming Bishop of Llandaff, then Salisbury, then Durham.
Shute founded England's first-ever cooperative shop at Mongewell
in 1794.

**LOTTIE BASE**           Born 1817, Standlake

**BLENDA BELCHER**        Born 1864, Chalgrove

EASTWOOD FITZ GEORGE LENNOX BIGGER   Born 1910, Headington

FLORENCE CRACKER                          Born 1878, Henley

SARAH CRAPPER BURKS                       Born 1841, Oxford

BILLY BUSTIN                           1820–1869, Oxford

MERCY CHAMP                            Married 1842, Oxford

## MARY ANN CRAPPER                   1820–1872, Woodstock

Members of the Bustin and Crapper family featured in a sobering list
in the letters pages of *Jackson's Oxford Journal* on Saturday, 5 July 1851.
In June, hard-hearted Mr Beckhuson had complained of the '21 able-
bodied men' who were sitting around doing nothing in the Oxford
Workhouse. One of the appointed guardians of the workhouse,
William Denyer, wrote a bitter reply on 3 July giving a full rundown
of the inmates and their almost total lack of able-bodiedness:

| | |
|---|---|
| W. Bramsccomb – | severe rupture |
| W. (Billy) Bustin, 15 years – | subject to fits |
| W. Crapper – | asthmatical |
| J. Claridge – | great debility |
| G. Field, sen. – | asthma |
| G. Field, jun. – | asthma, breast bone injured |
| T. Field – | affliction of the head |
| J. Hilsden, 60 – | feeble |
| F. Hayward, 60 – | dropsical |
| W. Hemming, sen. – | confirmed diarrhoea |
| W. Hemming, jun. – | affection of the heart |
| J. Hemming, 15 – | boy |
| W. Hedges – | deformed and ill |
| W. Harris – | diseased |
| G. Jackson – | able bodied |
| W. Mitchell, 16 – | boy, learning shoe-making |
| Frank Stephens, 60 – | imbecile |
| Bland – | a tramp |
| Drury – | diseased leg |
| Hairn – | not known |
| Johnson – | the itch |

Denyer's objection fell on deaf ears, however. In November that year, Billy Bustin and new inmate Bob Simpson were imprisoned for five days in solitary confinement 'for refusing to do the work set them at the workhouse'.

| | |
|---|---|
| **LIZZIE CAUGHT** | Born 1837, Headington |
| **JOHANNA CONQUER** | Died 1848, Chipping Norton |
| **FOSTER CUTBUSH** | Born 1830, Nettlebed |
| **GEORGE WEST HARDY DRY** | Born 1839, Oxford |

OSTA DYKE                          Married 1917, Woodstock

TOMMY FOAM                         Born 1812, Woodstock

ANNIE CANNON FRYER                 Married 1901, Woodstock

HAROLD HAREFOOT          Aka Harold I of England (1015–1040)
Harold Harefoot, son of King Cnut, was crowned in Oxford in 1035.
Legend says that he was actually the son of a cobbler, passed off as the
legitimate heir by Danish Cnut's Saxon wife Queen Ælfgifu, as Cnut
was unable to have children of his own. The 'Harefoot' nickname was
based on Harold's ability to move quickly on the battlefield.

LIZ CREEK HORE                     1820–1882, Lower Heyford

JOHN HUMAN                         Born 1804, Arncott

ELIZ JUCY KING                     Born 1826, Oxford

JOE KING                           1809–1872, Headington

ORIGINAL HERBERT LEE         Born and died 1879, Woodstock

CREWS LONG                         Born 1848, Witney

ADA LOOKER                    Born 1875, Cogges, Witney

LIZZIE MAGIC                       Born 1858, Horspath

HENRY NIX MAYDWELL                 Born 1895, Oxford

MABLE MELONY                       Born 1838, Holton

ISACC MOULDY                  Born 1806, Clifton Hampden

**YOUNG NEW**                          1842–1882, Bloxham

**MINNIE PANTING PANTING**            Born 1882, Witney
*Poaching Panting*: 'Thomas Panting and Edward Panting, charged with unlawfully entering Cornbury Park, armed with a gun for the destruction of game.' (*Jackson's Oxford Journal*, 1 March 1834)

**ALMEYED PAPER**                      Born 1836, Bampton

**AGAPE PARKER**                       Born 1875, Oxford

**HENRIETTA SILENCE PARSONS-GUY**      Married 1902, Thame

**JAMES WHIP PICKERING**               Born 1854, Headington

**WILL POWER**                         1818–1893, Deddington

**EMILY HOARE PRINCE**                 Born 1858, Oxford

**ERODAH RING**                        Born 1832, Cottisford

**JOHN RUBBER**                  Born 1800, Neithrop, Banbury

**TOMMY RUMBLE**             Born 1781, Goring-on-Thames

**MINNIE CROOK SHRIMPTON**             Born 1862, Thame

**SARAH SLOP**                         Born 1858, Islip

**REGISTER (OR REJESTER) SMITH**     1841, Tadmarton, Banbury

**SAM SAMWAYS SPICER**     Born 1840, Ascott-under-Wychwood

**MOSES SQUELCH**                      1809–1891, Henley

GAY STEFF                                      Born 1880, Oxford

SID STERN                                   1896–1918, Woodstock

JOHN STRANGEMAN                               Born 1826, Kingham

MASTER THOMAS STRONGITHARM                       Died 1798, Stonor

MARY JANE SWINDLER                          Born 1845, Woodstock

RICHARD LARGE TANNER                          1800–1880, Witney

ROB HONEY TOMBS                          Born 1877, Headington

FIENNES TROTMAN                          1752–1824, Bucknell

Trotman had estates at Bucknell in Oxfordshire, Siston in
Gloucestershire and in Northampton. Born into a landowning family
(but not a blue-blooded aristocrat), he was also MP for Northampton,
1784–90 (succeeding his uncle, another Fiennes Trotman). He was
described, with all the meanness of the Conservative press of the day,
as 'a little man who … was formerly a silk weaver but having lately
had a fortune of six or seven thousand pounds left him is living away
upon it'. This is a deliberately garbled version of the story, given that
Trotman was a rich landowner already. The family had been in the
cloth trade in the seventeenth century – no doubt the original source
of their wealth. Trotman's son and successor, yet another Fiennes
Trotman, graduated from Christ Church College, Oxford, and died
in 1835 aged 50.

ANNA URANIA TUCKWELL                          Born 1850, Witney

FRANK VIRGIN                             Born 1868, Headington

SARAH WEAKLEY                               1883–1949, Henley

# 6
# ALL WORK
# (AND SOME PLAY)

Many Oxfordshire names suggest ways of filling both work and leisure time. The following give some unhelpful clues as to the occupations, hobbies and achievements of their owners.

| | |
|---|---|
| THOMAS BETTS | 1820–1878, Thame |
| HANNAH BLEWITT | 1820–1908, Thame |
| EDWARD BOFFIN | 1820–1892, Banbury |
| THOMAS SAINT LAWRENCE HUNTER BOOKER | Born 1849, Wantage |
| LAKE CARTER | Born 1889, Filkins |
| REBECCA DREWETT | 1820–1888, Headington |
| JOHN DRINKWATER | 1820–1885, Banbury |
| VIRA TUSNIS DYER | Born 1906, Oxford |
| BORROWS CLUTTERBUCK | Died 1838, Henley |

## JOB COLLIER COLLIER

Born 1836, Rotherfield Greys

## JOHN FELL

Born 1770, Grove, Wantage

## CYCLE FORTESCUE

Born 1875, Caversham

## ELSIE MAY GOTOBED

Born 1901, Witney

*Gotobed has a blast*: On 28 March 1867, John Gotobed and George Connoway of Witney were injured while blasting rock at a local quarry. When the powder failed to explode they did the one thing that purchasers of fireworks have been warned against over the decades – they went closer to have a look, 'when it suddenly ignited, causing considerable injury to Connoway's hands and arms, and Gotobed's eyes and face'. (*Jackson's Oxford Journal*, 6 April 1867)

## HARRIET HADLAND

1820–1910, Bicester

## BETT HANDS

Died 1845, Banbury

## WILLIAM M. HANGMAN

Born 1821; at Worcester College, Oxford, in 1841 census

## SOLOMON HAWKES

1820–1899, Thame

## DUSTON RIKIN HEWER

Born 1864, Signet, Burford

## EMILY HICKS

1820–1901, Witney

## GUY GUNNING HUNTER

1890–1972, Henley

**LINE LAPPER**                                    Died 1839, Banbury

**LAWRENCE HEYORTH MILLS**                         Born 1837, Cowley

**WILLIAM MOBBS**                                  1820–1880, Banbury

**ELIZABETH NEWITT**                               1820–1885, Thame

**HILDA WEED OVERILL**                             Born 1886, Woodstock

**FREDERICK A. PAGE TURNER**                       1843–1931, Bicester

The Page Turner family was not without money and land, as this newspaper notice hints: 'Notice is hereby given, that all Persons who shall be found trespassing or killing Game on the Manors of Ambrosden, Wretchwick, Bicester, Market End, Merton, or Charlton, in the County of Oxford, which aforesaid manors are the Property of Sir Gregory Page Turner, Bart. will be prosecuted as the Law directs.' (*Jackson's Oxford Journal*, 23 August 1800)

**FOSTER PEAD**                        Born 1866, Warborough, Wallingford

**HEARTY PULLIN**                                  Born 1873, Witney

| | |
|---|---|
| ALICE MAY REASON | Born 1883, Chipping Norton |
| JAMES ROGERS | 1820–1907, Thame |
| RICHARD FISH SALTER | Born 1847, Oxford |
| ISABEL ELDER SKINNER | Born 1880, Oxford |
| MILLICENT HARDY SLATTER | Born 1892, Oxford |
| TEDDIE SLINGER | Born 1899, Chipping Norton |
| TEMPEST SLINGER | Married 1721, Oxfordshire |
| GEORGE NIX STONE | Born 1858, Bicester |
| DANIEL STOPS | 1800–1879, Thame |
| ELIZABETH WINSOR SWEATING | Died 1874, Banbury |
| KATHLEEN MAY TANTRUM | 1912–1995, Oxford |

## DAISY THATCHER
Born 1895, Henley

## ANNIE TOMBS TIPPING
Born 1919, Holton

## BENJAMIN TRAMPLETT
Married 1776, Abingdon

Benjamin Tramplett was an Abingdon maltster and coal merchant. His daughter, Mary Tramplett (1781–1867), along with her sister Anne (just 9 years old at the time), opened a boarding school in Abingdon in 1804. The following notice was posted in the local newspapers:

> The Miss Trampletts announce the Plan of establishing a BOARDING SCHOOL, for the instruction of YOUNG LADIES in polite Literature, their Father having entirely given up the House to them where they at present reside … Under these Circumstances they flatter themselves, that by a most assiduous Perseverance in the Improvement, as also combined with that of the most circumspect Attention to the Health, Morals, and Comfort of their Pupils, they sincerely hope to merit the Patronage and Support of those who may so far honour them as to consign to their Management the Education of their Children … Board, Education and Washing, £18.18s per annum … The School will open the 14th January, 1805.
>
> (*Jackson's Oxford Journal*, 20 October 1804)

## ISAAC KING TURNER
1834–1907, Fringford, Bicester

## RHODA TURTLE
Born 1843, Headington

## FORRESTER WRENCH WALKER
Born 1848, Bicester

## CHARLES BASSTOE WARDEN
Born 1882, Banbury

## HICKS WELLS
1712–1799, Hornton

## WILLY WALLY WHEELER
Died 1838, Woodstock

## NELLIE WIGGER
1891–1967, Oxford

## ALPHONSO HERRY WITHERS
Born 1868, Chipping Norton

## WALLY RING WORKMAN
Died 1840, Henley

## WILLIAM YELLS
1816–1850, Langford

William Yells, described in *Jackson's Oxford Journal* as 'Yeoman farmer of Faringdon' (seven miles south-east of Langford), had some of his chickens stolen by one William Major in February 1839. Major was imprisoned for three months.

# 7

# MONEY, MONEY, MONEY

It's a rich man's world … but not all the time. Oxfordshire's penny-pinching surnames range from filthy rich to dirt poor.

| | |
|---|---|
| PERCIVAL ROB DE BANKS | 1907–1986, Bullingdon |
| ERNEST JAS CASH | Born 1887, Caversham |
| CHARLIE CHANGE | Born 1846, Eye and Dunsden |
| ETHEL CROWN | Born 1886, Wheatley |
| JANE DOLLAR | 1876–1963, Banbury |
| FANNY DUCAT | 1836–1926, Pyrton, Henley |
| ELMOR FARTHING | 1817–1883, Oxford |
| WEALTHY GOULD | Born 1850, Witney |
| MARY GUINEA | Born 1826, Holton |
| STEPHEN H. HALFPENNY | 1889–1965, Henley |

| | |
|---|---|
| **HENRY KNAPP MONEY** | 1818–1891, Woodstock |
| **MIRANDA MONEYPENNY** | 1893–1929, Cowley |
| **IVA PENNY** | Born 1881, Headington |
| **MARTHA POOR** | Born 1791, Henley |
| **MARY ANN LARGE PRICE** | Born 1842, Witney |
| **LOVE SILVER** | Born 1859, Oakley, Thame |
| **IRVINE STERLING** | Born 1870, Oxford |
| **RICH SWELL** | Born 1771, Warborough |

**DICK LARGE TANNER**           1800–1880, Alvescot

Tanner was mentioned as 'constable of Alvescot' in a court case against a burglar in 1843. His evidence stated that the burgled property had 'appeared quite safe' on the evening before the crime, but that the following morning he had noted a broken window and – big clue – 'a ladder standing against the house'. A carpet, a blanket, a muff and a box of trinkets were the haul. In spite of Dick Large Tanner's evidence, the accused was found not guilty. (*Jackson's Oxford Journal*, 16 December 1843)

**SAM TENNER**           Married 1902, Henley

# 8
# THE GREAT OUTDOORS

Places, landscapes, moods – imagine a Constable or Turner
painting peopled with Marvel comic characters …

| | |
|---|---|
| PERCY LAKE ABSLOM | Born 1886, Chipping Norton |
| SARAH GRIFFIN T. BRIDGES | 1820–1896, Oxford |
| FREDDIE FREE BROOKS | Married 1869, Headington |
| FRIED BROOKS | Born 1898, Headington |
| JIMMY POND DUNN | 1818–1877, Witney |
| ALDRIDGE FIELD | Born 1831, Stadhampton |
| FANNEY FIELD | Born 1776, Kidlington |
| MARGRATE FOREST | Born 1839, Rotherfield Peppard |
| CHRISTOPHER CLOUD FORWARD | Born 1859, Henley |
| GEORGE SUNNOS GOODLAKE | Born 1848, Broadwell |

## URINA HEDGES    Born 1844 and married 1863, Chipping Norton

## ROSE ETTA HERITAGE                    Born 1871, Chalcombe

## HOPE HILL                             Born 1841, Sonning

## SEYMOUR HILLS                      Born 1886, Headington

## HENRY HOPE A. COURT INGLEFIELD          Born 1859, Henley

*Ingenious Inglefield*: On 23 June 1900, Oxfordshire brewing magnates the Morrells, of Headington Hill Hall, threw a party. Amongst the entertainers was a Miss Inglefield, who performed 'a thought-reading séance'. Blindfolded, she guessed various numbers and symbols, impressing the reporter of *Jackson's Oxford Journal*, but not fooling him. 'It is not for me to say how it was done. Mr Gandy [her assistant] does not speak to the lady, so there is no code. Some people think it can be really done through thought transference, but I am sceptical, and believe it is an extremely ingenious trick.' (*Jackson's Oxford Journal*, 30 June 1900)

## JAMES VALE JAMES                        Died 1847, Henley

## PERCY P. LEAVES                     1878–1959, Ploughley

| | |
|---|---|
| PRETTY LIGHT | Born 1901, Bix, Henley |
| CECIL NATAL MARSH | Born 1901, Cowley |
| FRANK EDWARD RACKSTRAW MOON | 1899–1975, Henley and Nettlebed |
| ROSE MOORFIELD | Married 1909, Headington |
| ADA MINNIE MOUNTAIN | 1904–1994, Henley |
| AMARIAH MOUNTAIN | Born 1826, Oxford |
| ERNEST HOPE OLDMEADOW | Married 1904, Bicester |
| ROSE POND | 1863–1932, Headington |
| BESSIE CRICK RIDGE | 1885–1981, Banbury |
| FANNY RIVERS | Born 1836, Rotherfield Greys |
| SARAH SCENERY | Born 1853, Kirtlington |
| CHARLIE SKIES | Born 1860, Churchill |
| PLEASANT SKY | Died 1865, Bicester |
| OCEAN SMITH | Born 1848, Headington |
| ANY WATERS | Married 1903, Banbury |
| WALLY WOODLAND | Born 1877, Burford |
| EARTH WORD | Born 1848, Headington |

# 9 AUDITIONING FOR THE PUNK ROCK BAND

Adopting a name worthy of a punk rock band –
Johnny Rotten, Sid Vicious, Rat Scabies, etc. –
was not just a 1970s phenomenon. Armed with a
time machine, the following nineteenth-century
worthies would all have been in with a good chance
of earning a footnote in the annals of punk rock.

| | |
|---|---|
| DICK BADMAN | Born 1839, Oxford |
| ARCHABALD BALLS | Born 1891, Hambleden |
| WILLY BALLS | Born 1874, Oxford |
| EDWARD GRIFFITH BASTARD, OF NORFOLK | Married 1926, Headington, |
| MAY BOGS | Married 1929, Banbury |
| CHARLIE CHUFF | Born 1852, Oxford |
| MARY CREATURE | Died 1843, Abingdon |
| KATE PRESTON DEVIL | Born 1836, Britwell Salome |

## JESUS DEVILHEART

Exact dates unknown, Oxford

Jesus Devilheart's real name was Joseph Vallard, a homeless man arrested at St Giles' fair in Oxford, 1888. Asked for his name, he replied, 'Jesus Devilheart, Marquis of Anjou, Commander of the forces of Heaven and Earth, Lord Mayor of London and Mayor of Oxford, descendent of Richard Coeur de Lion and the Plantagenets, William the Conqueror and Napoleon the First.'

## EMMA DOGGER

Born 1825, Headington

## HANNAH DUNG

Born 1888 Finstock, Chipping Norton

## FLOSSIE FREAK

Married Henley, 1903

## SAVAGE FRINCH

Born 1841, Oxford

## RAWSON GASH

Born 1850, Caversham

## LOUSY JEFFS

Born 1860, Banbury

## ANNIE MAY KILL

1904–1986, Ploughley

| | |
|---|---|
| Arthur Killer | Born 1828, Banbury |
| Ann Kilmaster | 1820–1894, Headington |
| Leah King | Born 1835, Benson |
| Win King | Born 1884, Henley |
| Archisalle Knife | Born 1891, Standlake |
| Jake Knife | Born 1802, Ducklington |
| Ed Mangle | Born 1806, Witney |
| Ellen Nickers | Born 1885, Neithrop, Banbury |
| Martha Pervey | Born 1851, Oxford |
| Fred Pimp | Born 1853, Bicester |
| Ed Ripper | 1910–1964, Ploughley |
| John Rubber | Born 1800, Neithrop, Banbury |
| Jane Rude | Married 1839, Bicester |

## JESSE SAVAGE SAVAGE

1837–1891, Woodstock

*Savage a-salt*: Sarah Savage was arrested in Abingdon on 15 March 1833: 'Sarah Savage, charged with stealing bacon and salted pig meat, the property of John Birch of Wallingford.' (*Jackson's Oxford Journal*, 16 March 1833)

## SEBRA SAVAGE

Born 1871, Chipping Norton

## MINNIE SCREECH

1876–1960, Witney

## WALLY SEWER

Born 1873, Banbury

## ELIZABETH SLAUGHTER

Died 1801, Oxford

## ERNEST RAPER

Born 1886, Oxford

## EDWIN RAPER SLAUGHTER

Married 1883, Oxford

## SID SMELL

Born 1888, South Leigh

## RACHEL SNIFF

Born 1854, Headington

## PRISCILLA STAIN

Married 1850, Banbury

## CHAS STENCH

Born 1864, Swerford

## MINNIE SUCKER

Born 1886, Thame

## ED ROCK TOMBS

Born 1881, Witney

## ROB TOMBS

1798–1869, Bicester

## ALF TRASH

1785–1822, Oxford

## GEORGIANNA TRASH

Born 1811, Oxford

## SAMUEL TRASH
1765–1838, Oxford

Grocer and Oxford councillor Samuel Trash was in trouble in 1801. 'All Persons indebted to the Estate of Mr Samuel Trash, Grocer, a Bankrupt, are desired immediately to pay the same without further Notice, into the Hands of Mr Joseph Andrews, Grocer, in the Corn market' (*Jackson's Oxford Journal*, 6 June 1801). But in 1823 Samuel Trash is back in business, selling 'Prepared chocolate, in pound and half-pound canisters' that 'possesses advantages far beyond any thing of the kind offered to the public, both on account of the facility with which it is prepared for table, as well as from its highly nutritive qualities' (*Jackson's Oxford Journal*, 18 October 1823). Sweet memory was all that remained in 1838: 'DIED. On Saturday last, at Summer Town, in the 73rd year of his age, Mr Samuel Trash, for many years an inhabitant of this city. He is sincerely lamented as an affectionate father and a kind friend.' (*Jackson's Oxford Journal*, 12 May 1838)

## ELSIE VILE
1900–1989, Headington

## JESSEE WHIP
Born 1854, Witney

## CLARKE WIDDLE
Born 1839, Banbury

## WILLIE WINDASS
Born 1815, Steeple Barton

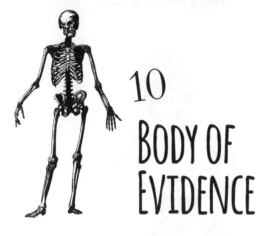

# 10
# BODY OF EVIDENCE

The human body has been the defining theme
of Western art since the Ancient Greeks.
Several Oxfordshire families have taken this theme
to heart … and face, and belly, and brain, etc.

| | |
|---|---|
| ED HEAD ALLITT | 1868–1888, Banbury |
| GERTRUDE OLIVE BALLS | Born 1892, Headington |
| HARRY DOUGHTY BALLS | Married 1886, Oxford |
| CHARLES BAREFOOT | 1820–1912, Headington |
| WORTHY BEAK | Born 1832, Broughton Poggs |
| WILLY BELLY | Born 1791, Claydon |
| CHATFIELD BLOOD | Born 1842, Cuddesdon |
| MINNIE BODY | 1882–1965, Oxford |
| CAROLINE SABINA BONE | Born 1885, Caversham |

| | |
|---|---|
| **BOB BOSOM** | Born 1776, Broadwell, Witney |
| **BENJAMIN BOWEL** | Born 1822, Sandford-on-Thames |
| **CALEB BRAIN** | Died 1839, Bicester |
| **IVOR BRAIN** | 1889–1964, Chesterton |
| **YOUNG BRAINE** | Born 1828, Charlbury |
| **CARRY BRAYNE** | Born 1876, Eynsham |

**AUGUSTUS HENRY BUST**                    Born 1882, Heythrop

**HEAD CHANDLER**                          Born 1855, Oxford

**ELSIE VIOLET CHEEK**                     1911–1980, Oxford

**ANNE HAIR EARLY**                        Born 1847, Minster Lovell

**KEZIA FACE**                             1810–1884, Witney

**ED FOOT**                                Born 1823, Banbury

**SWEYN FORKBEARD**                        960–1014

Sweyn Forkbeard, son of Danish King Harald Bluetooth, was King of Denmark and Norway, and became King of England in 1013. He made his mark on his briefly held kingdom by burning down Oxford. His son Cnut became king in 1016.

| | |
|---|---|
| **BOBBY GIBLETS** | Born 1889, Milton-under-Wychwood |
| **MARIE L. GIBLETT** | Born 1885, Milton-under-Wychwood |
| **THOMAS HEART** | Born 1786, Neithrop, Banbury |
| **ARCHIE KIDNEY** | 1913–1991, Oxford |
| **ELIZABETH ANN KNEE** | Married 1857, Witney |
| **JONA LEG** | Born 1860, Rotherfield Peppard |
| **ALFRED LUNG** | Born 1875, Woodstock |
| **PHILEMON RUMP** | Married 1866, Thame |

| | |
|---|---|
| ROSE ANNE SINUS | Born 1826, Oddington |
| ELIZA SMALLBONES | 1820–1903, Banbury |
| SARAH THUMBS | Married 1864, Henley |
| AUGUSTINE TOE | Born 1835, Witney |
| FLORENCE KATE TOES | Married 1892, Headington |
| FREDERICK CLOVIS TONGUE | Born 1903, Witney |
| LENA TOOTH | Born 1880, Blenheim |

# 11
# COLOURFUL PAST

Choosing a good family name is not always a black and white issue.

GREEN HILL BARN                    Born 1839, Adderbury East

JOHN GREEN BRAIN                    Died 1847, Bicester

JANE BLACK BROWN                    1877–1972, Bullingdon

HANNAH BLUE COW          Born 1833, Neithrop, Banbury

LOUISA E.M. DE REDD    Born 1835, Broughton Filkins, Witney

| | |
|---|---|
| EMMA GREEN DIX | Born 1855, Witney |
| GREEN GEORGE | Born 1836, Bensington |
| PINKEY GOLD | Married 1850, Witney |
| LEVI GREEN BODFISH GREEN | 1851–1865, Banbury |
| JONAS GREEN GREEN | Born 1882, Warborough |

A Narrow Escape – On Tuesday, a little child named Florence Green, of Signet, was admitted to the Burford Cottage Hospital, having narrowly escaped being burnt to death. It appears that Mrs Green's children were left alone in the cottage for a few moments, and that the little girl no doubt approached too close to the fire and her clothes ignited.

(*Jackson's Oxford Journal*, 20 January 1900)

| | |
|---|---|
| THOMAS WHITE HATT | 1815–1868, Chalgrove |
| JOHN BROWN JOHN | Born 1848, Oxford |
| EVA ORANGE | 1878–1949, Oxford |
| GEORGE FRED RED PARTRIDGE | Born 1903, Henley |
| PINKY PHIPPS | Born 1821, Witney |
| FANNY PINK | Married 1891, Henley |
| LETTY PINK | Born 1875, Caversham |
| WILLFRED BOURR PINK | Born 1869, Caversham |
| STAN PURPLE | 1921–1997, Oxford |

## ALBERT CHARLES WHITE WHITE RING     1858–1880, Wheatley

## SARAH FANNY BROWN ROADS     Married 1852, Oxford

## MARY SELINA WHITE RUFFELS     Born 1880, Denton

## GREEN TITCOMB     Born 1823, Burford

## MARY ANN WHITE WHITE     Born 1864, Oxford

## THOMAS ORANGE WIGINGTON     Born 1881, Oxford

## WHITE PIERCY WINNING     1845–1852, Witney

The short-lived White was not the first of his clan to bear that forename. White Piercy, born in 1702, had a son called White Piercy (born *c.* 1725). William White Winning, born in 1854, carried on the family tradition. The Piercy/Winning family was involved in the industry for which Witney was famous – blanket making.

## JANE YELLOW     Born 1876, Oxford

# 12
# HOUSE PROUD

Some people take the sentiment of 'home sweet home'
that little bit further – including all the fixtures and fittings.

| | |
|---|---|
| HENRY ALLEYWAY | 1820–1895, Henley |
| WILLIAM BANNISTER BANNISTER | Born 1905, Bicester |
| CORBETT BEDDING | 1915–1984, Ploughley |
| HANNAH BRICK | Born 1797, Kingham |
| LIZ CANDLE | Born 1795, Thame |
| JOSHUA ORION CASTLE | 1847–1874, Chipping Norton |
| ELIZA CHAIR | Born 1839, Henley |
| BEN COOKER | Born 1803, Neithrop, Banbury |
| MERCY SARAH COTTAGE | 1874–1969, Bullingdon |
| FRED CURTAIN | 1835–1894, Oxford |

| | |
|---|---|
| WILLIAM SHOLL STAIR DOUGLAS | Born 1870, Britwell Priory, Henley |
| ELIZA DRAIN | Born 1821, Oxford |
| ED DRAPES | Born 1817, Steeple Barton |
| ELSIE GERTRUDE DRESSER | 1889–1981, Witney |
| GARDEN DUFF | Born 1880, Great Haseley |
| RHODA J. HAY HALL | 1867–1940, Oxford |
| VILLA HALL | Born 1881, Bicester |
| GERTRUDE KATE HEATER | Married 1899, Oxford |
| HENRY HOBB | Born 1808, Henley |
| BATH ANNIE HORNSBY | Born 1836, Marston, Oxford |
| ALEXANDER HOVEL | 1857–1944, Oxford |

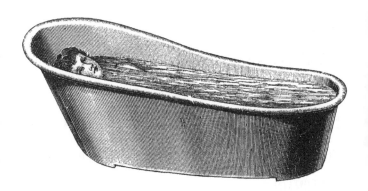

**DOREEN LOOS KITCHEN**  1920–1996, Ploughley

**FELIX LANDING**  Born 1818, Bampton

**MERCY LEATHERBARROW**  Married 1850, Banbury

Mercy's brother Thomas Leatherbarrow (born 1844) made the national press after being killed in London in June 1883. He was a cab driver, and died after being stabbed in the eye with a walking stick.

**FAITH LIGHT**  Born 1761, Swyncombe

**ANN MAT**  Born 1841, Middle Aston, Woodstock

**MARTHA OVENS**  1819–1876, Henley

**ALF ROOF**  Born 1849, Bicester

**EYRA ROOM**  Born 1838, Witney

**JOHN THAYLOR RUGG**  Died 1841, Headington

**BRIDGET SIDEBOARD**  1949–2004, Oxfordshire

**JIMMY TELLY**  Born 1834, Oxford

**LIDDLE TOWERS**  1918–1990, Ploughley

**MILLIE HAFE LIZZIE VICARAGE**  Born 1897, Chipping Norton

**TIMOTHY STONEHOUSE VIGOR**  1787–1812, Sunningwell

Timothy Stonehouse Vigor went to Oriel College and became rector at Sunningwell. He was also a Justice of the Peace at the Abingdon Assizes.

**WALTER WALL**  1841–1912, Eynsham

| | |
|---|---|
| PERCY ADOLPHUS WASHER | Died 1852, Oxford |
| FANCY WHALL | Born 1859, Thame |
| CHARITY WINDOWS | 1799–1874, Headington |

# 13

# GOODY GOODIES

During the eighteenth and nineteenth centuries there was a puritanical craze for austere, penitential names in some parts of England. Oxfordshire wasn't one of the worst offenders, but we still have a decent smattering of biblical references and holier-than-thou's.

| | |
|---|---|
| MERCY ABSALOM | Born 1848, Chipping Norton |
| SILENCE ADAMS | Born 1845, Banbury |
| ADELAIDE TRUTH ADAMS | Born 1837, Sandford-on-Thames |
| PATIENCE ADKINS | Born 1801, Banbury |
| PATIENCE ALLAWAY | 1791–1856, Henley |
| QUIET ALLWRIGHT | Born 1846, Cholsey |
| PLEASANT ARIS | Born 1821, Finmere |
| PRUDENCE ARTISS | 1820–1894, Chipping Norton |
| PROVIDENCE BAILDON | Born 1878, Goring-on-Thames |

| | |
|---|---|
| CHARITY BATT | 1820–1874, Headington |
| CHRIST PHON BERRY | Born 1891, Hanborough |
| TEMPERENCE BODEN | 1800–1868, Banbury |
| COMFORT BOSSOM | Born 1793, Headington |
| LIZZIE VIRTUE BRITTLE | Born 1873, Cowley |
| FAITHFUL CAPE | Born 1850, Oxford |
| HONOUR CHERRY | 1816–1893, Cropredy |

| | |
|---|---|
| **CONSTANT CLINTON** | Born 1876, Chipping Norton |
| **VIRGEN MARY COOPER** | Born 1785, Henley |
| **VIRGIN COOPER** | Died 1852, Henley |
| **MERCY CREED** | 1774–1851, Oxford |
| **IMMANUEL MAIDEN DAVIES** | Born 1845, Banbury |
| **SILENCE DAY** | Married 1849, Woodstock |
| **OPPORTUNE GANWRIT** | Born 1842, Shirburn |
| **CHRIST TUFF GEORGE** | Born 1821, and at St Mary Hall, Oxford in the 1841 census |
| **WILLIAM DECIMUS GODSON** | 1820–1898, Banbury |

**JOHN GOODENOUGH**          Married 1750, Oxfordshire

'Edmund Goodenough, for stealing a fagot, the property of Jos. Judd – to be imprisoned and kept to hard labour 14 days' (*Jackson's Oxford Journal*, 3 July 1847) … 'Henry Goodenough was summoned for allowing a cow to stray on the highway at Tetsworth, and was fined 5*s*, and 6*s* costs.' (*Jackson's Oxford Journal*, 13 December 1884)

| | |
|---|---|
| **LEZZIE GOODIN** | Born 1874, Cowley |
| **MERCY GREATREX** | Married 1867, Banbury |
| **FANNY SAINT GRIST** | Born 1840, Wallingford |
| **VIRTUE SEON SUSAN HALE** | Born 1874, Banbury |
| **JOB HOARE HONOUR** | Born 1845, Chipping Norton |

| | |
|---|---|
| VIRTUE M. INGS | 1882–1944, Ploughley |
| WILLIE VALANCE JUSTICE | Born 1883, Chipping Norton |
| MERCY KING LAMBALL | Born 1847, Headington |
| BLISS MANDER | 1790–1866, Banbury |
| ELIZA PERFECT MARLOW | Born 1890, Bicester |
| BRINSDON GOODCHILD MEADOW | Born 1902, Henley |
| CHRIST-GIFT NEWE | 1703–1727, died with her daughter in childbirth, Oxford |
| PRUDENCE PING | Born 1856, Middleton Cheney |
| PLEASANT PIPKIN | Born 1857, Horspath |
| BEAUTY POTTER | Born 1885, Henley |
| WISDOM SMITH | 1829–1906, Headington |
| UNITY STRAYLER, AKA SHAYLOR | 1829–1907, Leafield |
| BEST TOOLEY | Born 1881, Oxford |
| HONOUR WEARM TURRELL | Born 1834, Oxford |
| CHRIST WIGGINS | Born 1849, Burford |

## LAPIDOTH STRATTON WIGLEY
Born 1846, Wallingford

Lapidoth's one consolation was that she was not alone. Her siblings were named Theophilus (b.1841), Tryphena (b.1842), Tryphosa (b.1843), Philiplus (b.1844), Keturah (b.1846), and Philetus (b.1848). Their parents were Primitive Methodist ministers, and the names all have biblical roots.

## CHARITY WINDOWS
1799–1874, Headington

## SOLOMON WISDOM
Governor at Oxford Gaol in the 1780s

The poor state of Solomon Wisdom's gaol, situated in the city's ancient castle complex, caught the attention of Oxford's magistrates. They set about repairing and restructuring the site, appointing Daniel Harris (1760–1840) as Clerk of Works. He immediately fell out with Wisdom, one of the main disputes being the positioning of the prison dunghill. Wisdom was eventually sacked, losing his £20 a year salary, along with the money that prison governors extracted from their inmates before the gaol reform bills of the nineteenth century, including blackmail and the sale of alcohol.

# 14
# SEASONS
# GREETINGS

It's never too late or too early to celebrate some of
your favourite annual fairs, feasts and saints' days.

| | |
|---|---|
| RANDOLPH ST STEPHEN S. ADAMS | Born 1870, Oxford |
| SWITHIN ADEE | Died 1786, Oxfordshire |
| FRANK ST JOHN BADCOCK | Born 1854, Oxford |
| EASTER BALL | Born 1846, Epwell |
| EASTER BEACH | Born 1858, Henley |
| MARY CHRISTMAS | 1863–1929, Henley |
| MAY DAY | Born 1862, Watlington |
| VALENTINE DAY | Born 1912, Woodstock |
| ALICE CREDGINGTON EASTER | Born 1900, Oxford |
| COLTRIP ST MICHAEL GILBERT | 1886–1971, Banbury |

| | |
|---|---|
| **ARNIE HALLOWS** | 1887–1955, Oxford |
| **DON LENT** | 1924–2004, Oxfordshire |
| **MOSES MIDWINTER** | 1815–1878, Witney |
| **JOHN ST SWITHIN PEMBROKE** | Born 1879, Henley |
| **ST GEORGE STOCK** | Born 1850, Oxford |
| **ST ANDREW TYRWHITT** | Born 1876, Headington |
| **ED ST PATRICK WAINWRIGHT** | 1887–1977, Witney |
| **CHRISTMAS HENRY G.H. WINZAR** | Born 1886, Oxford |
| **MARINA YULE** | Born 1874, Oxford |

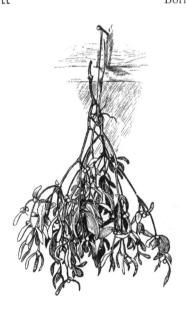

# 15

## DELUSIONS OF GRANDEUR

There might not be a single drop of aristocratic
blood in the family tree, but that has not deterred
some people from choosing names with a
less-than-subtle hint of toffery about them.

| | |
|---|---|
| EDWARD KING ATKINS | Died 1838, Banbury |
| PRINCE A.E. BELCHER | Born 1896, Blewbury |
| CLEOPATRA BOOKER | Born 1862, Headington |
| KING BRANDON | Born 1850, Thame |
| PRINCE FREDERICK BREAKSPEAR | Born 1886, West Hanney |
| HENRY KING BROWN | Born 1851, Thame |
| STEPHEN KING BROWN | Born 1849, Henley |
| PRINCE BULLER | Born 1911, Banbury |
| HENRY J. CAESAR | Born 1872, Heythrop |

| | |
|---|---|
| **PRESIDENT FERRICE CARR** | 1816–1900, Oxford |
| **PRINCE CARR** | Born 1826, Oxford |
| **KING GEORGE COLES** | 1919–2001, Oxford |
| **JAMES KING COPELAND** | Born 1819, Abingdon |
| **WILLIAM KING COPELAND** | 1804–1875, Abingdon |
| **CAESAR COXHEAD** | Born 1821, Westcot Barton |
| **NOBLE HALL DANCE** | Born 1868, Waterperry |
| **KNIGHTLY D'ANVERS** | Died 1740, Oxford |

Alicia D'Anvers, poet, and wife of Knightly, died on 13 July 1725 age 58. She was a remarkable woman, holding her own with the literary elite of the day. A translation of part of the lengthy Latin inscription on her monument at St Cross church, Holywell, Oxford, reads:

> She was a woman endowed with a ripe and lively wit, outstanding for her courage as for her compassion, learned without show, generous and devoted. She took the greatest pleasure in familiarity with literary people; she was invariably the only woman among them, but easily came up to the level of all of them, except that she was extremely wary of liberality with slander, and elegantly reined this in, seeing that she preferred to bear malicious talk than to retaliate … Knightly Danvers, Esq., raised this, in mourning, to his most beloved wife, much missed after almost thirty-eight years of marriage; and, if it had pleased Almighty God, he would gladly have chosen to live [no] longer and to die together with her; so now, following her example and her counsel, he hopes that he will meet her again in heaven.

Knightly D'Anvers was buried alongside Alicia in 1740.

| | |
|---|---|
| **DUKE DOWNES** | Born 1880, Letcomb Regis, Wantage |
| **RICHARD KING FOSTER** | 1819–1888, Bicester |
| **QUEEN GOSTELOW** | Born 1836, Bicester |
| **DUKE HALLETT** | Born 1895, Eynsham |
| **DUKE HAWKINS** | Born 1836, Oxford |
| **HAROLD KING HEDGER** | Born 1866, Abingdon |
| **JOHN PRINCE HOWSE** | Died 1840, Witney |
| **QUEEN F.M. HUTTON** | Born 1911, Henley |
| **PRINCE HENRY JEFFREYS** | Born 1839, Oxford |
| **DICK POPE JESTON** | 1826–1901, Henley |

KING ALFRED JONES      Born 1878, Drayton

AUGUSTUS KING LONG      1886–1984, Oxford

QUEEN ASIONY LOVERIDGE      Born 1834, Bicester

PRINCE A. MACE      Born 1870, West Hanney

NAPOLEON B. MAJOR      Born 1845, Standlake

JULIUS CAESAR MINETT      1816–1871, Henley

PHAROAH MOORE      1875–1913, Banbury

*More pharaohs*: Fined for selling low-fat milk! In January 1894 Jo Pharaoh was arrested for selling watered-down milk, and milk 'from which 30 per cent of natural fat had been abstracted'. He was fined 20*s* with 9*s* 6*d* costs. (*Jackson's Oxford Journal*, 20 January 1894)

OWEN ST JOHN MOSES      1873–1941, Oxford

FREDERICA LADY NORTH      Born 1840, Wroxton

PRINCE NORTON      1859–1867, Banbury

PRINCESS BEATRICE PALMER      Born 1886, Oxford

EDMUND KING PASH      Married 1839, Woodstock

HENRY PRINCE PEYMAN      1814–1877, Abingdon

KING CHARLES PORTER      1816–1908, Culham

PETER PRINCE PROWETT      Died 1769, Oxfordshire

MARY LADY RODD      1901–1981, Oxford

| | |
|---|---|
| LOUISA PRINCESS SMITH | Born 1887, Headington |
| KING THOMAS | Born 1841, Thame |
| LORD AGABUS B. THORN | Born 1898, Oxford |
| PRINCE PETER TINSON | Born 1877, Sutton Courtenay |
| JOHN KING TOMBS | Married 1838, Witney |
| PRINCE TUBB | Died 1836, an Oxford attorney |
| QUEEN ELIZABETH WEBB | Born 1897, Witney |

# 16

# Food for Thought

When a child is born, it is customary to gather family and friends and hold a celebration-cum-feast. Some Oxfordshire families have a headstart on the food element of the festivities.

| | |
|---|---|
| **WILLIAM JELLEY ADBY** | Born 1838, Henley |
| **ALDER COOK ADCOCK** | Born 1851, Headington |
| **AGNES AGGIS** | 1854–1920, Banbury |
| **LIZZIE BATE BACON** | 1820–1891, Headington |
| **MILICENT HARDY BACON** | Born 1892, Oxford |
| **ALECK L. BAKEWELL** | 1898–1948, Oxford |
| **ADELE BAP** | Born 1842, Faringdon |
| **GRISSEL BARRET** | Married 1664, Oxfordshire |
| **NELSON BEAN** | 1812–1881, Headington |

## ADOLPHUS SHARMAN BEER

1904–1983, Bullingdon
Thame and Oxford

Adolphus Sharman Beer died in Bullingdon. He was a physician, based at Radcliffe Infirmary, Oxford (amongst others), and a major in the Royal Army Medical Corps. There is a housing development in Thame named after him.

## CREWS BERRY

Born 1829, Headington

## JANE BISTO

Married 1842, Thame

## RICHARD PEAR BLAKE

Died 1856, Oxfordshire

## AGNES T. BONE

1871–1946, Banbury

## THOMAS EDWARD MAYO BOULTBEE

Vicar of St Cross,
Holywell, Oxford, 1943–1950

## MARIE PIE BOUVYER

Born 1867, Headington

## HATTIE BREAD

Born 1820, Abingdon

## FRANK BURGER

Born 1813, Standlake

## FAN BUTTER

Born 1868, Clanfield

## JANE CABBAGE

Born 1861, Thame

## HARDING CAFÉ

1850–1873, Bicester

## CHARLIE CAKE

Born 1857, Fawley, Henley

## GORG CAKEBREAD

Born 1840, Tadmarton

## MILDRED YOLANDE CANDY

Born 1889, Caversham

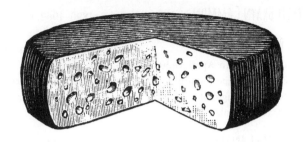

| | |
|---|---|
| **CHARLIE CHEESE** | Born 1861, Oakley |
| **ADOLPHUS CHERRY** | Born 1886, Garsington |
| **CRES CHERRY** | Born 1843, Milton-under-Wychwood |
| **LIZZY CHIP** | Born 1776, South Stoke, died 1847, Henley |
| **WILLIE CLARET** | Died 1843, Oxford |
| **BART COKE** | Born 1791, Goring-on-Thames |
| **JOE CRESS** | Born 1811, Chalgrove |
| **HORACE CURRY** | 1872–1944, Oxford |
| **SARAH CUSTURD** | Will dated 1772, Oxfordshire |
| **DONNIE DINNER** | 1913–1986, Oxford |
| **BETSY ANNE EGG** | Born 1831, Banbury |
| **ELLEN EGGS** | Born 1864, Oxford |
| **ANNE PANTER GAMMON** | Born 1822, Wallingford, married 1865, Thame |

## BERTIE BRAYN GAMMON
1890–1962, Oxford

## FRED BATTS GARLICK
Married 1903, Oxford

*Garlick crushed*: In April 1830, John Garlick of Abingdon was sentenced to three months' hard labour for bastardy. This crime involved fathering children out of wedlock, and doing nothing to provide for the child.

## HENRIETTA GARLICK
Married 1889, Headington

## EMMIE GERTRUDE GINGER
Born 1884, Neithrop, Banbury

## FANNY DUCKETT GRUBB
Born 1889, Neithrop, Banbury

## ETHEL HAGGIS
Born 1878, Cowley

## TOMMY HOGSFLESH
Married 1881, Headington

| | |
|---|---|
| JOHN EARLY JAM | Born 1811, Witney |
| CAROLINE JELLYMAN | 1820–1889, Banbury |
| CHARLIE BEAN KING | Born 1875, Banbury |
| CECIL JAMES KITCAT | 1865–1888, Headington |
| MARY LIVER | Died 1809, Stonor |
| ARCHIBALD MCBEAN | Born 1875, Rotherfield-Greys |
| PERCY MELON | 1893–1980, Wallingford |
| EDITH MARY MINCE | 1877–1878, Oxford |
| FLOSSIE MUFFIN | Born 1884, Headington |
| GEORGE CRISP MUMMERY | Born 1821, Rotherfield Greys |
| GERTIE IVE MUSTARD | 1883–1978, Oxford |
| JIM NUT | Born 1797, Shirburn |
| MARY ANN ONION | Born 1822, Headington |
| CHARLIE TALBUT ONIONS | 1874–1965, Headington |
| BECKY PICKLES | Died 1859, Oxford |
| FLORY PLUM | Born 1863, Oxford |
| SPICER PURDUE | Died 1806, Oxford |
| HENRIETTA SALMON | Married 1904, Chipping Norton |

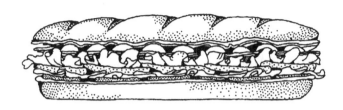

### BENJAMIN SARNEY
1702–1782, Rotherfield Greys

*Sarney sandwich!* 'John Sarney was driving a three-horse wagon from Bix to Henley on the 1st [January]. On the way back, near Rotherfield Grays, the horses bolted. Sarney was thrown from the wagon and sandwiched between the wheels and the road.' (*Jackson's Oxford Journal*, 5 January 1822)

### RICHARD SAUCE
Born 1838, Witney

### JAM SCARS
Born 1811, Henley

### EDITH FLORENCE SHERRY
Born 1870, Henley

### EVELYN B. TART
1902–1958, Oxford

### HERTA TRIMMINGS
Born 1893, Henley

### JAM TRIMMINS
Born 1776, Henley

### JESSIE TRIPE
1877–1958, Neithrop, Banbury

### VIOLET VEAL
Born 1898, Hook Norton

### LETTUCE VICHOTTS
Born 1896, Headington

### MILKY WARNER
Born 1773, Cote

| | |
|---|---|
| **George Whiskey** | Born 1830, Thame |
| **Fennell White** | Born 1776, Lewknor |
| **Tom Orange Wigington** | Born 1881, Oxford |
| **Willy Wine** | Born 1786, Drayton |

# 17 HUNGRY GIRLS

Best not to invite any of these girls to the banquet, however …

| | |
|---|---|
| **LENA ETTA BENCH** | 1910–1990, Banbury |
| **HENRIETTA BISHOP** | Died 1860, Banbury |
| **EMILY ETTA BOX** | Born 1859, Oxford |
| **BEATRICE ETTA BRIDGE** | Born 1888, Lyneham |
| **HENRIETTA CASTLE** | Married 1905, Oxford |
| **HENRIETTA CONSTABLE** | Married 1897, Banbury |
| **HENRIETTA CORNISH** | Married 1880, Henley |
| **EMMA, ELIZA AND JULIA EATER** | Born 1843/6/9, Hanborough |
| **HENRIETTA EELES** | Married 1918, Witney |
| **HENRIETTA FOOTE** | Married 1906, Witney |

| | |
|---|---|
| HENRIETTA FORTY | Married 1915, Headington |
| IVA ETTA GIBBONS | Born 1891, Banbury |
| EMILY ETTA GREENHALF | Married 1888, Witney |
| HENRIETTA HORN | Born 1850, Woodstock |
| HENRIETTA HUSSEY | Married 1897, Oxford |
| HENRIETTA MANN | Married 1902, Banbury |
| HENRIETTA MESSENGER | Married 1906, Headington |
| HENRIETTA NEWMAN | Married 1872, Headington |
| ETTA PAINTER | Born 1870, Banbury |

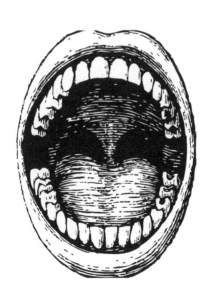

# MARRIAGE MADE IN HEAVEN

## 18

It's a great shame the pairs and groups in this section never met, as they were clearly made for each other.

**WASHINGTON T. HEAVEN**
1876–1954, Oxford

&

**GUNTHER HELL**
1905–1995, Oxford

**EDEN ADAMS**
Born 1845, Thame

&

**EMMA EVE**
1843–1922, Headington

**ANNIE E. LIFE**
1862–1952, Ploughley

&

**FRANK DEATH**
1877–1954, Oxford

**ARCHIBALD SPRING**
Born 1884, Oxford

&

**SELINA A. SUMMER**
Born 1874, Banbury

&

**HUGH AUTUMN COLES**
Born 1867, Banbury

&

**BARRINGTON WINTER**
Died 1845, Woodstock

## SIMS NIGHT
Married 1723, Oxfordshire

&

## ROSE FANNY DAY
Married 1888, Oxford

## ADOLPH PERISH
Born 1863,
Hambleden, Henley

&

## MARIE FUHRER
Born 1872,
Oxford

## EMILY RATTY
1832–1906,
Stonor and Pyrton

&

## JOE MOUSE
Born 1781,
Neithrop, Banbury

## RICHARD CHARLES DADD
Born 1843,
Chipping Norton

&

## CATHERINE MUMM
Born 1781,
Wootton-by-Woodstock

## NAPOLEON B. MAJOR
Born 1845, Standlake

&

## RUTH WELLINGTON
Born 1832, Ambrosden

## ED BALD
Born 1887, Cuddesdon

&

## COMFORT CURLEY
1855–1940, Oxford

## ERNEST MONEY
1880–1952, Oxford

&

## FRANK CASH
Born 1889, Bicester

## RICHARD ORPHAN
Born 1856, Eynsham

&

## FOSTER BOGGIS
Born 1897, Witney

**DIODATUS TAME**
Married 1694, Oxfordshire

&

**SIDNEY BOFFIN WILD**
Born 1888, Headington

**FANNY PANTING**
Married 1877,
Chipping Norton

&

**DICK PANTING**
Married 1868,
Chipping Norton

**FANNY STRIKE**
Born 1834,
Oxford

&

**WILLY STRIKE**
Born 1816, Stoke,
South Wallingford

**FANNY TOMES**
Born 1850, Banbury

&

**WILLY TOMES**
Died 1861, Headington

**CLARA PHYLIPPY TALL**
Born 1868, Oxford

&

**JAS SHORTER**
Born 1781, Cuddesden

**IVOR SANDALS**
Born 1905, Chipping Norton

&

**MABEL GRACE ARMINE SLIPPER**
Born 1866, Cowley

'A boy named James Raynham Slipper, in the employ of Dr Martin, was convicted, on his own confession, and sentenced to two calendar months' hard labour, for stealing, under very disreputable circumstances, a silver watch, the property of Emma Stevens, on the night and during the confusion of the fire at St. Helen's wharf [Abingdon].' (*Jackson's Oxford Journal*, 11 August 1860)

**ALFRED BATMAN**
Born 1873, Cowley

&

**ELFRIDA ROBIN**
1890–1986, Oxford

### IVOR STEED
1873–1939,
Chipping Norton

&

### WINNIE HORSE
Born 1796,
Minster Lovell

### IVOR SMALLCOMBE
Born 1880, Oxford

&

### ED HAIR
Born 1796, Lewknor

### ELIZA KEYS
Born 1796,
Eynsham

&

### EZEAKLE DOOR
Born 1824,
Shipton-under-Wychwood

### WILLIAM GARHELL BOW
Born 1827,
Oxford

&

### KATE M. ARROW
1894–1960,
Banbury

### ALAURA E. RICH
Born 1864,
St Thomas', Oxford

&

### THOMAS POOR
Born 1818,
Ipsden, Henley

### ESTHER HARRIET GIRL
1820–1892, Headington

&

### BILLY BOY
Born 1791, Henley

### MATILDA PHARAOH
1820–1891, Oxford

&

### CLEOPATRA ENDALL
Born 1789, Horley

### PRESILLIAN STOPS
Married 1702, Oxfordshire

&

### DOLATHA START
Born 1792, Eynsham

### CHARLES AVERAGE
1800–1872, Henley

&

### MEDIUM LIGHT
Died 1849, Henley

### ISAAC LOST
Born 1886, Oxford

&

### FANNY FOUND
Born 1855, Banbury

### ANN VAN
Born 1791,
Witney

&

### CAR CHERRY
Born 1841,
Milton, Chipping Norton

### RICH SALT
Born 1851,
Oxford

&

### DAISY DAGMAR PEPPER
Born 1881,
married 1911, Caversham

### FANNY FISH
Married 1861,
Banbury

&

### LIZZY CHIP
Born 1776, South Stoke,
died 1847 Henley

### ELIZABETH TEA
1792–1884,
Brize Norton

&

### NELLIE COFFEE
Born Caversham,
1892

# 19

# Animal Farm

Whether it's a taste for the wild life or a date with
John Farmer Giles (1881–1904, Witney), the biological
diversity of Oxfordshire's surnames is impressive.

| | |
|---|---|
| **Alfred A'Bear** | 1860–1934, Headington |
| **Edmund Ironsides A'Bear** | Born 1901, Headington |
| **Sarah Adder** | Born 1819, Eynsham |
| **William Otter Alcock** | Born 1821, Warwick, married 1865, Banbury |
| **Alf Hewett Badger** | Died 1852, Headington |
| **Harold Please Batts** | Died 1894, Witney |
| **Caroline A. Bear** | 1849–1888, Headington |
| **Edmund Whitfield A. Bear** | Born 1869, Henley |
| **Teddy Bear** | Born 1822, Rotherfield Greys |

## EDMOND BEAVERS
Born 1811, Cowley

Advert in *Jackson's Oxford Journal*, 5 December 1840: 'TEETH!! Mr Beavers, Surgeon Dentist … wishes particularly to call the attention of wearers of Artificial Teeth to his new description of Teeth, fixed without springs, ligatures, or wires, which never change colour nor decay, and so perfectly resemble the natural teeth as not to be distinguished from the originals by the closest observer. Letters addressed to Mr E. Beavers, Surgeon-Dentist, Lower Cowley House, Oxford, will receive immediate attention.'

## HENRY BUG
Born 1816, Little Tew

## MERCY BULLOCK
Married 1869, Thame

## DOT BUNNY
1890–1928, Headington

## EARNEST CATS
Born 1881, Kirtlington

## ABELARDO CHINCHILLA
Born 1895, Caversham

## DOMINGS CHINCHILLA
Born 1893, Caversham

## LOUSE COCKERILL
Born 1809, Launton

*Cock-a-doodle don't*: When Richard Cockerill's fifty-one sheep strayed and blocked the road in Middleton Cheney, he blamed his shepherd. The Petty Sessions that dealt with the issue were not impressed, as the shepherd on this occasion was a small boy. The boy had 'let them stray while he amused himself'. Cockerill was fined 10*s*. (*Jackson's Oxford Journal*, 4 June 1870)

## EMILY LEVERET CRAPPER
Born 1862, Oxford

## CHRISTIANA GIBBON DAY
Died 1864, Headington

## VIOLET DE WOLF
Born 1887, Henley

| | |
|---|---|
| EDGAR WANKLIN DOLPHIN | 1917–1993, Banbury |
| ELSIE DRAGON | 1914–1988, Oxford |
| DAVID ANT DUKER | Born 1861, Bampton |
| FOX FOX | Born 1837, Banbury |
| GEORGE GOAT | 1860–1883, Bicester |
| WOLF HARRIS | 1803–1874, Oxford |
| HENERY HORSE | Born 1821, Minster Lovell |
| WINNIE HORSE | Born 1796, Minster Lovell |
| JOHN H. JAGUAR | Born 1848, Chinnor |
| EDWARD RICHARD TURTLE KILBY | Born 1859, Chipping Norton |
| RACHEL HORSEY LAKE | 1790–1878, Oxford |
| CHARITY LAMB | Born 1860, South Newington |

| | |
|---|---|
| LYDIA LAMBKIN | 1857–1921, Woodstock |
| HARRIET LEOPARD | Born 1831, South Stoke |
| LIZZIE LION | Born 1793, Kingston Blount |
| GEORGE LIZARD | Born 1869, Shirburn |
| MICE WYATT LONDON | Born 1839, Oxford |
| REUBEN HIORNS MOLE | 1817–1885, Woodstock |
| HENRY MOOSE | Married 1858, Witney |
| MINNIE GERTIE MOTH | Born 1879, Henley |
| JOE MOUSE | Born 1781, Neithrop, Banbury |
| ANN OX | 1796–1848, Cropredy |
| SOPHIA PIGGIE | Married 1838, Oxford |

| | |
|---|---|
| EDNA MAUD RABBITT | 1905–1981, Oxford |
| ANN RAM | Died 1860, Chipping Norton |
| HATTIE RATTY | Born 1869, Henley |
| CLAPTON CRABB ROLFE | 1845–1907, Headington |
| LOUSE SKELEKER | Born 1825, Barton, Chipping Norton |
| ANN SWINE | 1852–1910, Headington |
| EDEN TURTLE | Born 1835, Combe, Woodstock |
| GEORGE WORM | Born 1847, Watlington |

## 20

# BIRDS OF A FEATHER

Flying high in the name stakes, we present:

**FLORENCE NIGHTINGALE BAILEY**                    Born 1856, Oxford

**HENNSEY KITE BEEAL**                    Born 1821, Swalcliffe

**DICKIE BIRD**                    Born 1845, Shenington
*Birds get the bird!* 'Commitments to our County Gaol … Daniel Bird and Edmund Bird, for feloniously stealing a fowl, the property of the Rev T. Fane.' (*Jackson's Oxford Journal*, 16 December 1837)

**BENJAMIN BUNTING**                    Died 1841, Witney

**REGINALD T.V.E. BUSTARD**                    Born 1896, Headington

**BERT BUZZARD**                    Born 1869, Oxford

**BOB CHICKEN**                    1884–1936, Banbury

**RHODA FINCH COSTER**                    Born 1881, Yarnton

**ALICE FLOEKHART CROW**                    1858–1876, Headington

| | |
|---|---|
| **THOMAS BIRD CROWE** | Born 1817, Ramsden |
| **SARAH SWIFT DEW** | 1815–1886, Bicester |
| **AQUILA DUCK** | Born 1858, Henley |
| **FANNY DUCK** | 1888–1964, Oxford |
| **HELENA SWEET EAGLES** | Born 1875, Oxford |
| **MIRABEL GERTRUDE M. FALCON** | 1883–1970, Henley |
| **CAROLINE AMELIA GEESE** | 1814–1891, Henley |
| **FANNY GOOSE** | Born 1827, Old Marston, Oxford |
| **DINAH GOSLING** | Born 1811, Brize Norton |
| **SPENER HAWKS** | Born 1816, Witney |
| **HERON HUDSON** | 1929–1999, Banbury |
| **PEREGRINE JACKSON** | Died 1850, Oxford |
| **ANNE DUCK JOHNSON** | 1833–1905, Headington |
| **CHARLES ROOK KNOTT** | Born 1857, Headington |
| **WILLIAM STARLING LARK** | 1911–1999, Henley |

## LOTTIE LINNET

Born 1871, Whitchurch-on-Thames

## WILLIAM MALLARD

Born *c.* 1437, Oxford

A seal bearing the words *SIGILLVM GVLIELMI MALARDI CLERICI* ('the seal of William Mallard, clerk') was unearthed during the laying of the drains for All Souls College in 1437. This may have been the origin of the Hunting the Mallard ceremony, a drunken All Souls festival so rowdy that it is only allowed to be staged once every 100 years (with the next one due in January 2101). Revellers led by a Lord Mallard, carrying a duck (dead in 1901, wooden in 2001) on the end of a long stick, parade the college grounds hunting for a mythical giant mallard. The first of these 'mallards' to be hunted may have been William, owner of that lost medallion; but with lashings of beer and folklore thrown at it over the centuries, the true origins of the tradition will never be known for sure. The event's unique Mallard Song is still sung at All Souls College gaudies (feasts), and contains several ear-bending verses, including:

> *The Griffin, bustard, turkey and capon*
> *Let other hungry mortals gape on*
> *And on their bones with stomachs fall hard,*
> *But let All Souls' men have the Mallard!*

| | |
|---|---|
| Bartholomew Sparrow Montgomery | 1820–1850, Headington |
| Septimus Nightingale | Died 1848, Henley |
| Fanny J. Ostrich | 1881–1941, Oxford |
| Elizabeth Wren Panting | Married 1882, Witney |
| Benjamin Seymour Parrott | Born 1883, Woodstock |
| Hugh Ivor Partridge | Born 1906, Begbroke |
| Patience Pigeon | 1830–1904, Neithrop, Banbury |
| Thomas Cuckoo Rawbone | 1791–1853, Oxford |
| Izard Wildegose Rogers | Born 1888, Oxford |
| Esther Rook | 1702–1786, Oxford |
| Henry James Swallow Slatter | Died 1852, Oxford |
| Shadrach Sparrow | 1835–1906, Oxford |

## LOVEDEN SPARROWHAWK
Born 1886, Witney

## BLANCHE I. STARLING
Born 1783, Caversham

## JOHN DUCK SWEETING
1827–1858, Faringdon

'MELANCHOLY AND FATAL ACCIDENT – It is with regret that we have to record the death of Mr John Duck Sweeting, aged 33 … The unfortunate deceased was attending to the brewery of his aunt at the Craven Arms Inn, Hungerford … He accidentally let a candlestick fall into the vat and on reaching over to recover it his feet slipped, the stool on which he stood being wet, and he was precipitated head foremost into the boiling water … (He lingered) in the most excruciating agony until Monday, when he died.' (*Jackson's Oxford Journal*, 13 November 1858)

## JUDATH TURKEY
Born 1805, Milcombe

## SUSANNA WALLDUCK
1800–1876, Bicester

## CATHERINE EAGLE WIDDOWS
Born 1854, Bampton

## ELIZABETH WILDGOOSE
Married 1655, Oxfordshire

## IZARD WILDEGOSE THE YOUNGER
Died 1810, Oxford

## IZARD WILDGOOSE THE ELDER
1694–1784, Denton and Cuddesden

## FANNY A.A. WOODCOCK
1864–1949, Oxford

# 21

# SOMETHING FISHY

Much as I love seafood, I'm pleased that
I don't have to carry it with me wherever I go.
Which is exactly what the following folk had to do.

## HANNAH BODFISH
1820–1868, Tadmarton

Hannah Bodfish's elder brother James Bodfish (born 1805) of
Tadmarton near Banbury was one of many farm labourers who, fearing
their livelihood was threatened by the increasing mechanisation of
farming, decided to destroy the opposition. He was jailed in Oxford
in December 1830 with four others for 'having at Tadmarten [*sic*]
feloniously destroyed a threshing machine … also destroyed a hay-
making machine'. (*Jackson's Oxford Journal*, 11 December 1830)

## ED BREAM
Born 1871, Steeple Barton

## MARY FISH BREDIN
Born 1845, Banbury

## FISH (OR FYSHE) BURGES
1766–1845, Oxford

## ETHELVY EARLY CHUBB
Born 1876, Cogges, Witney

## ALFRED CHARLES COCKLE
Born 1893, Cowley

CAROLINE E. CODLING — Born 1888, Cowley

ROSETTA DACE — Born 1848, Blenheim, Woodstock

FLORENCE FLANCH EELY — Married 1888, Oxfordshire

JOHN FINS — Born 1840, Oxford

FANNY FISH — Married 1861, Banbury

ROBUSTIA MARIA FISH — Born 1868, Oxford

A. BABY FISHER — From 1901 census, Chipping Norton

ELXISE ADELAIDE GILL — Married 1856, Headington

ANNIE GOBY — Born 1850, Steeple Aston

HERBERT H. GUDGEON — Born 1876, Ipsden, Henley

CONSTANCE HADDOCK — Born 1870, Headington

*Jackson's Oxford Journal* reported on the sad fate of another Haddock, far from home: 'Major R. Haddock, of the 67th Regiment, killed during an elephant hunt at Ceylon, 27th June – the wounded animal seized him round the body, threw him on the ground, and trampled him to death.' (*Jackson's Oxford Journal*, 29 November 1828)

ELI HAKE — Born 1855, Cowley

ESTHERA HERRING — Born 1854, Blackthorn, Bicester

ROWLAND HERRING — Born 1798, Thame

FANNIE LAMPREY — Born 1853, Bodicote

| | |
|---|---|
| LEINELL LAMPREY | Born 1841, Neithrop, Banbury |
| ALFORD DAVID HATCH LING | Born 1882, Chinnor |
| DICK LAMPREY LOVELL | 1800–1874, Banbury |
| GERTRUDE MULLET | 1863–1947, Ploughley |
| DICK PERCH | Born 1812, Shiplake |
| JAMES GREEN PIKE | Born 1821, Watlington |
| WILLIAM HIFFE PIKE | Born 1837, Wheatley |
| NELLIE PLAICE | Born 1883, Oxford |
| DECIMA RAY | Married 1854, Oxford |
| RODA ROACH | Born 1814, Thame |
| HEDWORTH LAMPTON ROE | Born 1901, Oxford |
| BOWER BERTRAM RUDD | Born 1915, Witney |
| PRISCILLA LIDDELL SALMON | Died 1859, Oxford |
| MARY SHARK | Born 1860, Caversham |
| ISAAC GEORGE SKATE | Born 1828, Crowmarsh Gifford |
| ADA BOSS SOLE | Born 1890, Neithrop, Banbury |
| FANNY SPRATT | 1814–1851, Farnborough |
| JOHN TENCH | 1766–1848, Great Rollright |

### ERNEST TROUT
1882–1945, Oxford

### FRED TURBOT
Born 1864, Banbury

### EUSEBIUS WHITING
1812–1835, Oxford

## 22

# HERBACEOUS BORDERS

Whether hedging their bets or in blooming health,
there were plenty of green-fingered names in the county.

| | |
|---|---|
| PANSY IRIS AHRENS | 1914–1986, West Oxfordshire |
| IVY ALDER | Married 1915, Oxford |
| IVY ASH | Married 1920, Oxford |
| ELDER R. BANYAN | Born 1898, Cowley |
| BERNIE BIRCH BARLOW | Born 1886, Henley |
| BLANCHE VINE BARNEY | Born 1894, Thame |
| PRUDENCE ASH BERRY | Born 1847, Headington |
| VINE CLINTON BIRTIE | Born 1836, Oxford |
| NEWMAN BRIER | Born 1844, Steeple Aston |
| JAS BURDOCK | Born 1811, Bradwell, Burford |

**MARTIN FOLKES BUSH** Born 1859, Oxford, married 1882, Bicester

**DAHLIA LORELLE BUTTERFIELD** Born 1889, Oxford

**LIZ HERB CHURCH** Born 1885, Thame

**LEONARD FLOWER CLAPPEN** Born 1886, Witney

**MONICA THORNE CLOVER** 1910–1995, Henley

**CHARLES OAK CRISP** Born 1878, Henley

**SNOWDROP VIOLET DUNK** Born 1886, Newhaven, Sussex, married 1910, Henley

**LOVE FOREST** Born 1883, Charlbury

**IVY GARDNER** Married 1920, Banbury

| | |
|---|---|
| WALLY GRASS | Born 1886, Wootton-by-Woodstock |
| GEORGE BEECH GUISE | Born 1895, Henley |
| GEORGE STRANGE HEDGE | Born 1847, Neithrop, Banbury |
| BECKY HERBS | Born 1786, Witney |
| BETA HOLLYHAWK | 1790–1866, Chipping Norton |
| BOADICEA VIOLET HUGHES | Born 1886, Oxford, married (and became Boadicea Beesley), 1908 |
| THISTLE HUNT | Born 1889, Oxford |
| SAGE JEWITT | Died 1847, Headington |
| CHARLIE BEAN KING | Born 1875, Banbury |
| DAISY CROSS LARDNER | 1912–1994, Oxford |
| MARY MARJORAM | Born 1885, Headington |
| GRASS MOIRA | Married 1886, Thame |
| IVY U.B.D.B. MORTIMER | Married 1913, Headington |
| MERCY MOSS | Died 1841, Bicester |
| ALBERT LENTON BEECH MURRAY | Born 1900, Headington |
| GRASS MURRAY | 1825–1895, Henley |
| ELIZABETH ELIZA PINE | Born 1852, Oxford |

| | |
|---|---|
| LOUISA VALLIE PLANT | Born 1863, Bicester |
| BENJAMIN PRIVET | Born 1831, Black Bourton |
| VEON ROOT | Born 1804, Wardington |
| LILY ROSES | Born 1882, Churchill |
| LEAFY SMITH | Born 1797, Bicester |
| FLOASY VIOLET SOLLOWAY | Born 1890, Headington |
| EDITH BLANCHE SPRUCE | Born 1889, Oxford |
| ROSE FLOWER STRUDWICK | Born 1875, Oxford |
| CHARLIE TREE | 1873–1943, Banbury |
| NELLY TREES | Married 1916, Oxford |
| WALLY TULIP | 1911–1967, Banbury |
| MOSSE WALTER | Born 1815, Northmoor |
| AGNES G. WEED | 1844–1915, Headington |

## 23

AVE!

Latin names were popular in the eighteenth and nineteenth centuries – redolent of Ancient Rome and classical heritage, and appealingly out of place amongst the powdered wigs and top hats of Georgian and Victorian Oxfordshire.

| | |
|---|---|
| **ALBIN ARIES** | Born 1845, Chipping Norton |
| **DECIMUS ALCOCK** | 1807–1889, Banbury |
| **CLAUDIUS BELCHER** | Born 1874, Curbridge |
| **REGULA BURNET** | Born 1898, Oxford |
| **CIRCE CHIVERS** | Born 1898, Oxford |
| **SEPTIMUS CLUTTERBUCK** | Born 1864, Banbury |
| **ALBANUS, BERNARDUS AND CAROLUS DEARLOVE** | Born 1836/5/8, Stonor |
| **VENUS HUCKIN** | Born 1841, Chadlington |

## Hercules Humphreys                      1698–1800, Eynsham

On Saturday last died, at Ensham, in this county, Hercules
Humphreys, in the 102nd year of his age. This remarkable man
retained the full use of his faculties to the last, and was subpoenaed
on evidence on a trial in this City in the 101st year of his age.
Of his surviving children the eldest is 78 and the youngest only
seven years old.

(*Jackson's Oxford Journal*, 27 September 1800)

## Tertius William Jack                    Born 1910, Thame

## Sextus George Lees                      1887–1984, Bullingdon

## Dido Margan                             Born 1862, Oxford

## Scholastica Messenger                   Born 1882, Headington

## Firnrick Hercules Mortimer              1885–1898, Bicester

## Octavius Ogle                           1829–1894, Oxford

## Hercules S. Porteus                     Born 1860, Headington

## Drusilla Quarterman                     Born 1835, Garsington

## Frank Vulcan Reading                    Born 1863, Banbury

## Aeneus Seary                            Born 1828, Combe

## Agrippa Small
Born 1816, Watlington

## Exuperious Turner (or Turnor)
Died 1840, East Challow

'At the last Assizes … in Abingdon, Exuperious Turnor and John Buck Shepherd were found guilty … for conspiring to destroy Game in the night, on the estate of Thomas Goodlake, Esq. at Letcombe Regis.' Six other accomplices were being hunted down, 'part of a desperate gang of poachers'. Turner was no itinerant vagabond, though – the son of another Exuperious Turnor, they both had licenses to hunt game, and Turnor junior became a landowner himself, inheriting from his father the Mansion House and extensive lands at East Challow near Letcombe. No stranger to trouble, however, in August 1828 he was forced to sell 'pursuant to a Decree of the High Court of Chancery' as part of legal proceedings 'Coster against Turnor'. He died in 1840. (Quotes from *Jackson's Oxford Journal*)

## Amrose Octavius Tustian
1848–1915, Banbury

## Mars Wakelin
Born 1893, Headington

## Ulysses Walker
Born 1859, Banbury

## Vita Castitia Walker
1874–1903, Headington

## Henry Cornelius Agrippa Willis
1754–1843, Longcot

Advertised his services as 'carpenter etc.' in *Jackson's Oxford Journal*.

# 24
# WEATHERING

The child–parent relationship can often be a little stormy.
The Met Office has issued warnings for the following:

| | |
|---|---|
| GOODWIN G. BREEZE | 1874–1963, Henley |
| JUSHUA JONES COOL | Born 1837, Hook Norton |
| ROBINA DICKSON COOLER | 1913–1992, Henley |
| REUBEN COOLING | Born 1853, Churchill |
| FOSTER ELEMENT | Born 1870, Hailey, Witney |
| SUSAN FOG | Born 1809, Holwell |
| KATHERINE FANNY FROST | Born 1872, Cowley |
| WILLY HAIL | Born 1821, Oxford |
| MARY HOT | Born 1854, Oxford |
| SUSAN HOTTER | Born 1831, Henley |

| | |
|---|---|
| SUNNY JORDAN | Born 1936, Ploughley |
| ETHEL WIND IVES | Born 1886, Headington |
| EVA LIGHTENING | 1902–1982, Oxford |
| JOHN MIST | Born 1869, Cowley |
| GRACE RAIN | Born 1870, Caversham |
| GEORGE WILLIAM PRUDENTIA RAINBOW | Born 1851, Banbury |
| MAY SLEET | Born 1864, Banbury |
| TEMPEST SLINGER | Married 1721, Oxfordshire |
| HARRIET O.O. SNOW | 1837–1919, Eye and Dunsden |

| | |
|---|---|
| MARGARET STORM | 1844–1943, Banbury |
| PLEASANT SUMMERS | Married 1862, Bicester |
| SARAH SUN | Born 1820, Littlemore, Abingdon |
| WILFRED P. THUNDER | 1912–1927, Henley |
| ELIZABETH WARM | Born 1828, Brize Norton |
| CLARRISE M. WARMER | Born 1888, Shiplake |
| WILLY WARMER | Born 1789, Neithrop, Banbury |
| SARAH WETTER | Born 1819, Banbury |
| CATHERINE M. WIND | Born 1822, Steeple Aston |

# To Name or Not to Name, That is the Question

## 25

When Shakespeare walked into a pub and was told 'You're bard', he could not have foreseen the consequences of his outpourings on the parish registers of eternity. The following people have gone through life with a little hint of Will power.

| | |
|---|---|
| CORDELIA ATTWOOD | 1796–1857, Eynsham |
| JULIET BAUMGARTNER | Born 1864, Nettlebed |
| CAROLINE MACBETH BIRD | 1796–1881, Headington |
| STANLEY BOLINGBROKE | Born 1882, Oxford |
| ERNEST BOTTOM | 1886–1953, Oxford |
| DESDEMONA BOWELL | Died 1849, Headington |
| ROMEO CAMPOLI | 1862–1940, died Ploughley |
| PORTIA CARTER | 1776–1846, Headington |
| TROILUS CLARE | 1857–1915, Clanfield |

| | |
|---|---|
| TITUS CLUTTERBUCK | Born 1839, Henley |
| ROBERT AMRAPHEL ANDRONICUS GROVE COLLEY | Born 1859, Banbury |
| CLEOPATRA ENDALL | Born 1789, Horley |
| OPHELIA FUSE | 1781–1857, Watlington |
| HAMLET HORATIO GILLAM | Born 1877, Headington – married 1904 in Abingdon, died there 1961 |
| BRUTUS BERTIE HOLLEY | Born 1889, Oxford |
| RADNEY MUNDY LEAR | Born 1866, Oxford |
| CLARA E. MacDUFF | Born 1866, Burford |
| TOM OTHELLO MARKS | Born 1879, Henley |

**JULIUS CAESAR MINETT**                    1816–1871, Henley

**EDITH CRESSIDA PEACH**            Born 1881, Shipton-on-Stour,
Warwickshire, married 1905, Banbury

**TIMON PHELPIS**                          Born 1841, Chalgrove

**CORIOLANUS ROWLES**                      1894–1987, Ploughley

**WILLIAM SHAKESPEARE**                 Born 1801, North Stoke

**NOEL HENRY PLANTAGENET SOMERSET**    Born 1886, Headington

**AGNES BEATRICE TEMPEST**                 1882–1971, Banbury

**CORDELIA THICK**                         1869–1947, Henley

**HORATIO DE VILLE TILLING**        Born 1872, Chipping Norton
… The nearest Falstaffs, Cymbelines and Shylocks are in Middlesex!

# 26
# BEHIND CLOSED DOORS

Names can hint at all manner of close encounters of the
rude kind. Here's a quick look at What the Butler Saw
(possibly Thomas Hardaway Butler, born 1851 in Oxford),
before we come to the really rude bits!

| | |
|---|---|
| **AMBROSE ACOCK** | Born 1819, Chipping Norton |
| **MARY ANN ACOCK** | Born 1848, Chipping Norton |
| **TOTTIE MAY BELLMAN** | Born 1888, Ploughley |
| **FLOSSIE BINT** | Born 1887, Tackley |
| **LIZZY BUSTY** | 1844–1904, Witney |
| **WILLY CRUSH** | Born 1901, Bletchingdon |
| **CORNELIUS CRUTCH** | Married 1851, Witney, and died there in 1864 |
| **ANY CUMINGHAM** | Born 1871, Oxford |

| | |
|---|---|
| ANN CURVEY | Born 1849, Witney |
| EDWARD CHARLES GOBBLE | Born 1862, Bicester |
| CONSTANT HORLOCK | Born 1865, Oxford |
| CLARA LAURA KNOCKER | Born 1856, Oxford |
| LOVEDEN LANSPREY | Born 1838, Woodstock |
| ALICE BISHOP PAINTER | Married 1907, Witney |
| S. QUELCH (SARAH) | 1812–1888, Headington |
| VIRGIN RUMBLE | Born 1838, Henley |

## MELONY SCOBELL                    Born 1835, Rotherfield Greys

## MARCUS ELEAZER ERT SLAPOFFSKI                    Born 1825, Oxford

Slapoffski was head of an Oxford Jewish family living on St Aldates –
the street that had been the backbone of Oxford's Jewish sector prior
to the expulsion of the Jews in 1290 (at which time it was known as
The Great Jewry). There were actually two, unrelated, Oxford fami-
lies with the name Slapoffski, the other headed by Adolph (born in
Oxford, 1827). Marcus and Adolph united as The Hungarian Brothers,
or Slapoffski's Band, to perform music at shows in Oxford and beyond.
Neither was actually Hungarian – Marcus was born in Holland,
Adolph in Latvia. It also appears that Marcus Eleazer Ert adopted the
Slapoffski surname in order to form the 'Brothers' band with Adolph.

## ANN GOMM STOCKINGS                    Born 1856, Chipping Norton

## WILLIAM TOTTIE    Canon of Christchurch in the 1780s and '90s

## JOSEPH STRIPPER TREACHER                Born 1816, Headington

## TOMMY TUGWOOD                          Died 1841, Bicester

## ROWLAND TUGWOOD                        Born 1838, Burford

Poor Rowland Tugwood was not happy with his lot. On 30 November 1856, 'Rowland Tugwood, apprentice to Mr T. Hall, plumber and glazier, of Burford, was charged with absconding from the service of his master; ordered to return.' (*Jackson's Oxford Journal*, 6 December 1856). On 12 September 1857: 'Rowland Tugwood, apprentice to Mr T. Hall, was charged with leaving his service; the indentures were ordered to be cancelled.' (*Jackson's Oxford Journal*, 19 September 1857)

## 27

# Oo-er, Sounds a Bit Rude

Some rude names are unavoidable, on account of an existing surname loaded with *Carry On*-esque innuendo. Others are plain unforgiveable. If you don't know what the poet Philip Larkin said Mums and Dads do to us, look it up on the Internet now, and then marvel at the following:

| | |
|---|---|
| **Thomas John Acock** | Born 1838, Oxford |
| **Elizabeth Adcock (E. Adcock)** | Born 1828, Headington, and another in Thame, same year |
| **Ellen Allbutt** | Born 1816, Oxford |
| **Richard 'Dick' Allnutt** | 1804–1857, Oxford |
| **Elizabeth Arscott** | 1820–1886, Headington |
| **John Thomas Badcock** | 1819–1873, Oxford |
| **Sarah Howard Badcock** | 1820–1872, Headington |
| **Betty Bare** | Born 1872, Banbury |

| | |
|---|---|
| **WILLY BEARD** | 1789–1867, Henley |
| **ALICE BEAVERS** | 1820–1899, Headington |
| **ALFRED MING BELCHER** | Born 1881, Henley |
| **DICK BENT** | 1863–1900, Banbury |
| **EDWARD COX BIRD** | 1820–1904, Thame |
| **DICK BLOWS** | 1876–1957, Ploughley |
| **RAYMOND C.P. BOLLOCK** | Married 1945, Oxford |

## ADA BONER
Born 1884, Dorchester on Thames

## DICK BRAIN
1791–1869, Westcott Barton

Richard Brain's brother, John, was arrested for 'feloniously receiving three trusses of stolen hay' from incorrigible hay-makers Thomas Barratt and William Eadle in June 1843. Dick was one of the witnesses. The judge decided that, with so much hay and straw lying around, it was impossible to ascertain whether the suspicious trusses had been stolen or not. Its nomination for dullest court case of the year was never in question, however. (*Jackson's Oxford Journal*, 1 July 1843)

## FENN BUMPASS
Born 1883, Dorchester on Thames

## DICK BURGERS
Born 1852, Oxford

## DICK BUSTIN
1826–1862, Oxford

In September 1843 Dick Bustin, of St Ebbe's Street in the long-gone slums of Oxford, was arrested for stealing apples from a garden in St Giles and imprisoned for ten days (*Jackson's Oxford Journal*, 9 September 1843). Poor Bustin committed suicide on Monday, 3 February 1862. He was found 'in the privy with his throat cut in a dreadful manner, and a razor lying by his side. Surgical assistance was immediately sent for … At that time the man was not quite dead, but as the head was nearly severed from the body all efforts to save him were to no avail.' The jury returned a verdict of temporary insanity. (*Jackson's Oxford Journal*, 8 February 1862)

## BERTIE BUTT
1876–1918, Headington

## MARY WELLS BUTT
1830–1902, Headington

## BETTIE M. BUTTOCK
Born 1880, South Stoke

## FLOSSIE BUTTS
Born 1882, Headington

**ADA COCK**           Born 1894, Milton-under-Wychwood

**AMELIA VICTORIA CHAMBERLAIN COCK**      Died 1841, Banbury

**JANE COCKBILL**           1800–1885, Oxford

**ANN COCKHEAD WILLIS**           Born 1872, Witney

**JOSEPH COCKHEAD**           1791–1847, Long Hanborough

**WILLY COCKHEAD**           1790–1871, Long Hanborough

In March 1800 at a hearing in Oxford's Town Hall, 9-year-old Joseph Cockhead was imprisoned for six months for stealing fourteen loaves of bread. Joseph Cockhead spanned the generations in Long Hanborough, with further boys of that name registered in 1800, 1834, 1840 (d.1915) and 1866 (d.1934), all related to the briefly imprisoned Cockhead.

**TITTY COLEMAN**          Born 1868, Chipping Norton

**JAM COX**          Born 1821, Henley

**MERRY COX**          1880–1905, Bicester

**NORA COX**          1895–1932, Henley

**RHODA COX**          1879–1968, Headington

*A fishy tale of Fanny and Cox*: John Cox and his friend Frank Slatter 'were charged with illegally fishing at Grandpont, on 27th March'. A policeman had seen them 'fishing the water there with a rod and snare attached to it'. However, Cox's landlady Fanny Sims provided an alibi, saying that she saw Cox 'all day' on the 27th, and he had not left the house until the evening. As a result of her evidence, the case was dismissed. (*Jackson's Oxford Journal*, 14 May 1881)

## Charley Seymour Cox
Born 1868, Ipsden, Henley

## Charlie Coxhead
Born 1879, Henley

## Job Coxeter
1847–1926, Headington

## John Coxeter
1761–1844, Cassington and South Leigh

*Coxeter fails to keep house!* 'William Keep and Charles Howse, charged with feloniously breaking open the dwelling house of John Coxeter, of South Leigh, and stealing therefrom divers articles of wearing apparel.' At the same hearing they were charged with stealing from two others, and sentenced to death. (*Jackson's Oxford Journal*, Saturday, 6 March 1830)

## Bert Willy Crack
Born 1887, Thame

**WILLY CRAMP**                1884–1973, Oxford

**WILLY CRUTCH**        1806–1883, Wootton-by-Woodstock
'William Crutch, Edward Crutch [and four others] were indicted for a riot at Wootton, near Woodstock, on the 24th of November. They all pleaded not guilty.' They were, however, found guilty and fined 20*s* and ordered to 'keep the peace' for twelve months. (*Jackson's Oxford Journal*, 8 January 1831)

**WILLY CUMMING**                1869–1950, Ploughley

**HENRIETTA CUMMINS**        Died 1850, Headington

**ELIZA DIX**                1820–1875, Oxford

**HENRIETTA DIX**        Married 1926, Witney

**MIKE ANDY FANNY**        Born 1816, Chipping Norton

**MARY JOHN FECKER**        Born 1816, Launton

**DICK FILLER**        Born 1833, Lewknor

**ROSY FISTER**        Born 1863, Towersey

**DICK FLUX**                1820–1905, Witney

**AH FOOK**        1886–1918, Headington

**EMILY HENRIETTA SETITIA FOOKS**        Born 1845, Thame

**ERNEST FUCHS**                1909–1993, Oxford

**EMILY LOUISA FUGGETT**        Married 1901, Banbury

IVER GASH                              1890–1978, Oxford

WILLY GIRL                         1786–1862, Headington

ANN A. GOODHEAD               Born 1825, Headington

ADA BESSIE GREATHEAD             Born 1880, Oxford

**DICK AND WILLY HAIR**          Born 1838 and 1840, Lewknor

**CARNAL HALL**          Born 1844, Headington

**WILLIE HANDCOCK**          1800–1883, Headington

**DICK HARD**          Born 1829, Shutford West, Banbury

**WILLY HARD**          Born 1836, Witney

**KATHLEEN A. HARDCOCK**          Married 1933, Banbury

**MARY HARLOT**          Married 1839, Henley

**DICK HEAD**          Born 1831, Whitchurch-on-Thames

**FANNIE HISCOCK**          Born 1873, Kidmore End

*Hiscock throws a wobbly*: Charlie Hiscock was riding to Wantage, seated on one of the leading horses of a coach and four. All was going well until they reached a hill 'on the road leading from the Red House to the Wobbley Downs' (which you'll struggle to find on an Ordnance Survey map). On the downhill journey, Hiscock's horse stumbled and fell. The coach kept on going, crushing both man and beast. A few hours later, when Hiscock's father was passing by the spot, Charlie's battered body was finally rescued. He was, however, dead. (*Jackson's Oxford Journal*, 20 January 1900)

**JAMES BONER HUMPHRIES**          Born 1847, Little Milton

**ISAAC HUNT**          1806–1890, Oxford

**WALTER MIKE HUNT**          Born 1895, Headington

**WILLY HUNTER**          1870–1935, Oxford

**ERIC FOWKES HYMAN**          Born 1911, Tiddington

| | |
|---|---|
| **WILLY JELLY** | Born 1844, Bloxham |
| **CHARLES KNOBB** | 1841–1901, Nettlebed |
| **ELIZA KUNT** | Born 1849, Wheatley |
| **HENRY LE NOB** | Born 1874, Cowley |
| **ED LICKER** | Born 1833, Caversham |
| **DORIS TUGELA LUSTY** | Born 1900, Caversham |
| **WILLIE MANUEL** | Born 1877, Oxford |
| **WILLY MOUNTIN** | Born 1801, Toot Balden |
| **ROBERT COXETER NUTT** | Died 1859, Bladon |

*Bringing home the bacon*: In 1838 Henry Berry was imprisoned 'for stealing 200lbs weight of bacon, the property of Robert Coxeter Nutt of Bladon'. (*Jackson's Oxford Journal*, Saturday, 20 January 1838)

**CARRY ORGAN**                                        Born 1890, Headington

| | |
|---|---|
| MARY ANN PECKER | Born 1854, Banbury |
| MARY PENIS | Born 1901, Chipping Norton |
| WILLY PLANK | Born 1811, Oxford |
| ROBBY WILLY BUTT POLE | Died 1895, Oxfordshire |
| WILLIE PORK | Born 1825, Bix |
| WILLY PULLEY | Born 1870, Caversham |
| MARY A. PUSSEY | Born 1834, Oxford |
| WILLY RAM | 1797–1885, Headington |
| WILLY RIDER | Born 1841, Henley |
| DICK RIMMER | 1908–1985, Banbury |
| WILLY RISING | 1907–1947, Headington |
| DICK ROGERS | 1833–1904, Headington |
| WILLY ROOTS | 1805–1877, Bicester |
| JANE RUDE | Married 1839, Bicester |
| DICK SAUCE | Born 1838, Witney |
| WILLY SHAVE | Born 1892, Banbury |
| JAMES SHITTY | Born 1787, Ducklington |
| WILLY SMALLPIECE | Born 1874, Eye and Dunsden |

| | |
|---|---|
| **MINNIE SUCKER** | Born 1886, Thame |
| **WILLY SWELL** | 1848–1909, Oxford |
| **JOHN THOMAS** | Born 1843, Witney |
| **WILLY TIME** | Married 1661, Oxfordshire |
| **MARIE C. TIT** | Born 1884, Headington |
| **LIZZY TWOCOCK** | Married 1845, Oxford |
| **WILLY WEEDON** | Born 1854, Chalgrove |
| **WILLY WICK** | 1881–1949, Oxford |
| **HILDA MUFF WILKINS** | Born 1896, Chesterton |
| **WILLY WITHERS** | 1796–1871, Cowley |

# 28 FANNY POWER!

It's not fair, you cry, to laugh at the name Fanny,
bestowed so innocently all those decades ago!
Well, that might be true … but (adopts Sid
*Carry On* James laugh) it's still a giggle, isn't it?

| | |
|---|---|
| FANNY ACOCK | Born 1871, Idbury, Chipping Norton |
| FANNY ADCOCK | Died 1849, Headington |
| FANNY HUTT ASH | Died 1846, Headington |
| FANNY BADCOCK | Born 1849, Oxford |
| FANNY BAKER | Died 1843, Bicester |
| FANNY BALLS | 1847–1925, Chipping Norton |
| FANNY BANNISTER | 1820–1998, Headington |
| FANNY BATTS | Died 1857, Witney |
| FANNY BEAK | Died 1846, Witney |

| | |
|---|---|
| **FANNY BEARD** | 1881–1940, Oxford |
| **FANNY BEAVER** | 1886–1959, Shiplake |
| **FANNY BELCHER** | 1864–1914, Witney |
| **FANNY BIGGERS** | Born 1806, Witney |
| **FANNY BIGGERSTAFFE** | Died 1857, Thame |
| **FANNY BISHOP** | Died 1857, Banbury |
| **FANNY BLED** | Died 1853, Woodstock |
| **FANNY BLISS** | Died 1845, Woodstock |
| **FANNY BOFFIN** | 1823–1893, Stoke Lyne |
| **FANNY BOWL** | 1838–1914, Witney |
| **FANNY BOYLES** | Died 1854, Thame |
| **FANNY BRAIN** | 1875–1960, Oxford |
| **FANNY BRAYNE** | Died 1841, Banbury |

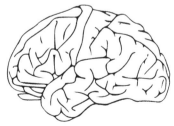

## FANNY BREWER Died 1852, Oxford

*Trouble brewing*: On 28 July 1882, 8-year-old Fanny Brewer of Cholsey was left in charge of her 2-year-old brother Ernest while their parents went out to work. According to the report in *Jackson's Oxford Journal*, Ernest had a bad back and was unable to stand. His sister wheeled him outside in a pram, leaving him in the care of her younger sister, who pushed the pram into a shed 'and left the child sitting there by the side of a tray of water' while she went to play with friends. The tray was used for washing, and was eight inches deep. When she returned from sweeping the cottage, Fanny found that poor Ernest had fallen from the pram and drowned.

## FANNY BUCKETT Born 1832, Henley

## FANNY BUCKLE Died 1850, Thame

## FANNY BUDD Born 1861, Woodstock

## FANNY BUM Born 1839, Binfield Heath

## FANNY BUNNING 1819–1892, Woodstock

## FANNY BUNTING Born 1838, Banbury

## FANNY BUSH Born 1876, Caversham

## AMY FANNY BUTTER Born 1887, Henley

## FANNY CATCH Born 1832, Cropredy

## FANNY CATERER Born 1926, Thame

## FANNY CHALLIS Born 1850, Nettlebed

## FANNY CHAMPION Born 1856, Caversham

| | |
|---|---|
| **FANNY CHERRY** | Born 1852, Headington |
| **FANNY CHICK** | Married 1840, Bicester |
| **FANNY CLEAVER** | Born 1926, Hook Norton |
| **FANNY COOK** | Died 1860, Thame |
| **FANNY COX** | Died 1860, Thame |
| **FANNY CRABB** | Born 1803, Oxford |
| **FANNY LEARY CRACKNELL** | Born 1838, Oxford |
| **FANNY CRAPPER** | Born 1841, Chipping Norton |
| **FANNY CREAMER** | Born 1877, Thame |
| **FANNY CRUTCH** | Born 1826, Wootton-by-Woodstock |
| **FANNY CURRY** | Born 1856, Hanborough |
| **FANNY DAY** | Married 1840, Headington |
| **FANNY DIPPER** | 1835–1909, Witney |
| **FANNY DIX** | Died 1852, Witney |
| **FANNY DUNKIN** | Born 1846, Thame |
| **FANNY DYER** | Born 1801, Hanborough |
| **FANNY FIDDLER** | Born 1861, Enstone |
| **FANNY FIRMIN** | Born 1837, Henley |

| | |
|---|---|
| FANNY FISHER | Born 1866, Oxford |
| FANNY FLOWERS | Born 1856, Banbury |
| FANNY FOREST | Born 1872, Witney |
| FANNY FRIEND | 1831–1911, Great Tew |
| FANNY FULLER | Born 1858, Thame |
| FANNY GALLOP | Born 1834, Hardwick, Witney |
| FANNY GARDENER | 1793–1870, Oxford |
| FANNY GOTOBED | 1832–1916, Witney |
| FANNY GUNN | Born 1840, Banbury |

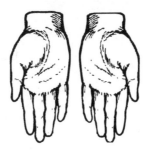

| | |
|---|---|
| FANNY HANDS | 1810–1887, Banbury |
| FANNY ETTA HATTON | Born 1904, Banbury |
| ROSA FANNY HEDGES | 1852–1882, Headington |
| FANNY HICKS | Born 1869, Forest Hill |
| FANNY HITCHCOX | Born 1842, Middleton Cheney |
| FANNY HOARE | Married 1838, Witney |
| FANNY HOLDSWORTH | Died 1856, Bicester |
| ANNIE FANNY HONEY | Born 1872, Headington |
| ROSE FANNY HONOUR | Born 1898, Headington |
| FANNY HOWSE | 1820–1901, Chipping Norton |
| FANNY HUCKIN | Died 1850, Chipping Norton |
| FANNY HUNT | Born 1835, Witney |

*Wedding bells in Witney*: On 8 August 1854 Fanny Hunt married Bob Gotobed, on the same day as Willy Pumfrey from the Wagon and Horses pub marred Elizabeth Beckinsale of the Black Head pub.

| | |
|---|---|
| FANNY ING | 1846–1925, Thame |
| FANNY JACOCKS | Born 1844, Banbury |
| FANNY KEEN | 1828–1876, Oxford |
| FANNY A. KING | 1860–1888, Thame |
| FANNY C. KING | 1872–1924, Headington |
| FANNY LAPPER | 1799–1876, Wendlebury |
| FANNY LARGE | Born 1819, Kencott |
| FANNY LEAK | Born 1859, Souldern |
| FANNY LEAVER | Died 1854, Thame |
| FANNY LINES | Born 1851, Chipping Warden |
| FANNY LODGE | 1847–1936, Chipping Norton |
| FANNY LORD | Born 1825, Eynsham, |
| FANNY LOVEGROVE | Born 1848, Banbury |
| IDA FANNY MAYCOCK | Born 1905, Banbury |
| FANNY MERRY | 1837–1920, Oxford |
| FANNY MILLER | Born 1849, Wardington |
| FANNY MOLE | Born 1866, Steeple Aston |
| FANNY MONUMENT | 1873–1943, Ploughley |

| | |
|---|---|
| **Fanny Mould** | Born 1845, Banbury |
| **Fanny Nash** | Born 1806, Hook Norton |
| **Fanny Nutt** | 1869–1950) Neithrop, Banbury |
| **Fanny Needle** | Born 1846, Woodstock |
| **Fanny Organ** | 1855–1951, Oxford |
| **Fanny Pain** | Born 1816, Caversham |
| **Fanny Painter** | 1797–1864, Bicester |
| **Fanny Parker** | 1851–1929, Rotherfield Greys |
| **Fanny Peachey** | 1854–1912, Filkins |
| **Fanny Petts** | Born 1854, Bicester |
| **Fanny S.Potts** | Born 1833, Banbury |
| **Fanny Pounder** | Died 1854, Wantage |
| **Fanny Power** | Born 1849, Deddington, Woodstock |
| **Fany [sic] Power** | Born 1898, Banbury |
| **Fanny Price** | 1799–1853, Oxford |
| **Fanny Puddle** | Born 1851, Chipping Norton |
| **Fanny Rogers** | 1834–1912, Headington |
| **Fanny Rumble** | Born 1839, Eye and Dunsden |

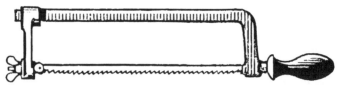

| | |
|---|---|
| FANNY SAW | Died 1848, Woodstock |
| FANNY SHEPHERD | 1820–1911, Headington |
| FANNY SLAUGHTER | 1856–1925, Oxford |
| FANNY SOLLIS | 1846–1923, Woodstock |
| FANNY SPICER | 1785–1872, Banbury |
| FANNY SPRING | Born 1860, Enstone |
| FANNY STEED | Married 1837, Chipping Norton |
| FANNY STEW | Born 1870, Oxford |
| FANNY STOKER | 1830–1904), Woodstock |
| FANNY STONE | 1869–1960, Oxford |
| FANNY STOPS | 1808–1871, Thame |
| FANNY STREET | Born 1852, Henley |
| FANNY THATCHER | 1881–1955, Henley |
| FANNY VENTERS | Born 1805, Bloxham |
| FANNY WALKER | 1844–1898, Bicester |

| | |
|---|---|
| **FANNY WATERS** | 1806–1891, Banbury |
| **FANNY WEAVER** | Married 1839, Witney |
| **FANNY WELLS** | 1855–1931, Chipping Norton |
| **FANNY WHETTON** | Born 1858, Adderbury East |
| **FANNY WINDOWS** | Born 1835, Cowley |
| **FANNY WOODCOCK** | Born 1802, Witney |
| **FANNY WORLD** | Born 1816, Fulbrook |
| **FANNY WRENCH** | 1877–1959, Oxford |
| **FANNY WYLLIE** | 1846–1937, Ploughley |

# 29 THE GUEST LIST FROM HELL

In spite of the many pigeonholes opened up in this
book, not all historic Oxfordshire's wonderful family
names can be so easily categorised. The following
kids have just one thing in common – parents
who can't be trusted with a birth register.

EDGAR WILLIAM A'BEAB          Born 1885, Headington

MARTHA BURRUP ABEL          Born 1847, Banbury

JOHN NIMLE A'BIAR          Died 1840, Oxford

THIRZA CILSTINE ABRAHAM          Born 1859, Woodstock

REGINALD BRODIE DYKE ACLAND          Born 1856, Oxford

ADA UARANIA ADAMS          Born 1877, Banbury

FANNY ADAMS   Lots of them, including one born 1796 in Oxford

ANN E. ADNAMES          Born 1841, Henley

MAUD MARY FRYER AFFORD · Born 1860, Headington

LUCY PROFFITT AINGE · 1856–1887, Banbury

ONE ALLEN · Born 1806, Filkins

HILLYER ALLWRIGHT · Born 1871, Cholsey

SHAH CROSS ALLWRIGHT · 1874–75, Henley

GEORGE SIX AMES · Married 1859, Banbury

GRAC ANDERSAN · Born 1830, Nettlebed

MANASSER ARSIC · *c.* 1130–1190 of Cogges Manor, Witney
Eleventh-century Manasser Arsic, Sheriff of Oxfordshire and Berkshire, was in the second wave of Norman landowners following the Conquest in 1066. He passed his lands to his son Robert, who in turn bequeathed them to his son, a second Manasser Arsic (1130–1190), High Sheriff of Oxfordshire and Berkshire 1160–1162.

WARE PLUMPTRE AUSTIN · 1842–1907, Headington

BARBE BAILLEY · 1837–1918, Bicester

HENRY ATKINS BANGER · Born 1809, Steeple Aston

ANN DILL BARBY · Born 1830, Alvescot, Witney

CADWALLADER COTAR COKER BECK · Born 1820, Crowell

SERINGA LYDIA BENWELL · 1820–1906) Headington

APPOLONIA WILHELMINA BIGUS · 1925–1986, Henley

| | |
|---|---|
| McMORRELL PECEASED HATE BLEECK | Born 1812, Oxford |
| THOMAS ELDERFIELD BOSSOM | 1820–1893, Headington |
| ALIAS BOX | Born 1841, Oxford |
| GRACE CREIS BRISCOE | Born 1857, Neithrop, Banbury |
| QUEENIE TOPSY BROADAWAY | 1907–1990, Ploughley |
| AMELIUS JOHN TEN BROEKE | At Magdalen Hall in the 1841 census |
| CARBET BUSWELL | 1781–1841, Adderbury |
| ROLAND GEORGE OVER BUTT | Born 1876, Headington |
| CLAUDIUS ROLAND CHIPCASE | 1905–1972, Henley |
| LIFELY CLARKE | 1781–1843, Witney |
| ELIZA NORTH COBBLEDICK | Born 1850, Oxford |
| HERBERT MOSELY COCKSEDGE | Married 1887, Bicester |
| ER COMPTON | Born 1846, Neithrop, Banbury |
| THEODOSIA COOCH | 1847–1880, Henley |
| URANIA ETHEL COOKE | 1892–1984, Bullingdon |
| CHARLES FORTY COULING | Born 1853, Oxford |
| STANLEY GEORGE DUDE COVEY | Born 1897, Oxford |

### Trevilliam Fortuna Costigon Cox
Born 1864, Witney

### Flave Restinde Dayman
1800–1872, Headington

### Falkes de Breauté
Sheriff of Oxfordshire and Berkshire, died 1226
Falkes de Breauté was Sheriff between 1215 and 1223. He was a loyal defender of kings John and Henry III, and his heraldic symbol was a griffin. His London residence was called Falke's Hall, which became Fawkes Hall, then Foxhall, Fauxhall and, finally, Vauxhall. Vauxhall cars began production at Vauxhall Ironworks in 1903 and in a time-defying piece of symbolism the company still uses Falkes de Breauté's griffin as its heraldic badge.

### Digby Delamotte
Born 1779, Oxford

### Edward Batt Dolley
Died 1848, Witney

### Dustaee Dunan
Born 1843, Banbury

### Methuselah Eaton
Died 1839, Witney

### John England England
Born 1901, Banbury

### Honsee J. Eustace
Born 1875, Nettlebed

## New Dalrymple Fanshawe

Born 1818, Henley (and still called New on the 1871 census)

## Ford A. Ferge

Born 1668, Swalcliffe

## Jane Old B. Ferme

Born 1898, Oxford

## Saint Frideswide (or Fritheswithe)

*c.* 650–757, pre-Oxford Oxford

One of the contenders for the title 'Founder of Oxford', with a suitably weird name. Frideswide was the daughter of local royalty; and according to legend she summoned divine intervention to blind some violent pursuers, and to create St Margaret's Well (aka the Treacle Well) at Binsey. She founded a nunnery on the site that later became Christ Church College in Oxford.

## Florence Frogley

1857–1923, Headington

*Indebted to Frogley*: 'All Persons indebted to the Estate of Mr James Juggins, late of the City of Oxford, deceased, are desired to pay their respective Debts immediately to Mr William Frogley, at Mr Juggins' late Residence, or they will be sued without further Notice – Oxford, 21 March 1800.' Juggins had died in June 1799 and was buried at Cuddesden. (*Jackson's Oxford Journal*, 22 March 1800)

| | |
|---|---|
| **EDEN GIFKINS** | 1820–1882, Thame |
| **ANNA GRAM** | Born 1811, Ambrosden |
| **LEVI GUBBINS** | 1820–1897, Woodstock |
| **AUGUSTA GUNTRIP** | 1820–1885, Thame |
| **HENRY HASH** | Born 1860, Witney |
| **PATRICK MAHERSHALAHASHBAZ HEAD** | Born 1865, Neithrop, Banbury |

Mahershalahashbaz was a name given to the second son of the prophet Isaiah in the Bible, translating as 'He has made haste to the plunder', reflecting Isaiah's conviction that the Assyrian King Tiglath Pileser III would crush both Damascus and Samaria, and that these countries' alliance was therefore not a threat to Judah.

| | |
|---|---|
| **ANY HELS** | Born 1891, Oxford |
| **HARTIE HERITAGE** | 1876–1953, Launton |
| **LEONARD HERITAGE-LITTER** | Born 1919, Bicester |
| **CORNWALL HITCHCOX** | 1800–1877, Banbury |
| **HARTY JOHN HITCHCOX** | 1878–1965, Banbury and Chipping Norton |
| **NELLIE VIOLA HOBRO** | Born 1880, Oxford |
| **MANY HORRIDGE** | Married 1876, Henley |
| **LOOKERISHA HULL** | Born 1856, Cowley |

## CHRISTIANA SOPHIA FANNY HELY HUTCHINSON

Died 1843,
Oxford

## SOP HYALD

Born 1828, Ascott-under-Wychwood

## ALPHA IMBUSCH

1863–1935, Oxford

## ENSEBY ISHAM

Died 1745, Oxfordshire

## CRIC JAKEMAN

Born 1885, Sandford-on-Thames

## MARATHON BEATRICE JAMESON

1889–1981, Oxford

## WALLY JEMMAT

Married 1676, Oxford

## EMLEY JETT

Born 1840, Headington

*Unlawfully misbehaving?* On 5 February 1842: 'On Thursday last Edward Jett was convicted before the Rev. N. Dodson, of unlawfully misbehaving himself in the service of Mr Henry Lipscombe, of Wytham, and sentenced to 21 days' hard labour in the house of correction.' (*Jackson's Oxford Journal*)

## BARZILLA JONES

Married 1717, Oxfordshire

## MONA OGLA CONNIE KNIGHT

Born 1909, Steeple Barton

## HOBE LINES

Born 1847, Chipping Norton

## L.L. MELOW LITTER

Born 1852, Bicester

## VANGBEN OGLE LOCKE

Born 1891, Banbury

## KIMPTON MABBET

Married 1712, Oxfordshire

## ARTHUR PHOSPHOR MALLAM

Born 1872, Headington

JOHN RANALGH DE LA HANT MARETT          Born 1900, Oxford

LITTIE BETURES LOUSE MILLIN          Born 1898, Ramsden

NARK NEAL          Born 1834, Northmoor, Witney

ELIZ 3 PARKER          Born 1821, Hethe, Bicester

THYRSA GAGE PART          Born 1873, Launton

WELLINGTON RENTON PASCOE          Born 1857, Oxford

LARRY SPRUCER CHEWALIER PEARCE          Born 1902, Combe

CONSTANCE ANY PEASLY          Born 1886, Cuddesdon

CONDD PERRIN          Born 1834, Fringford

CHRIS CRISS PHILLIPS          Born 1883, Thame

OFFSPRING THOMAS PLAISTER  Born 1839, married 1872, Oxford

FRANCIS PONKING          Died 1847, Wallingford

Ponking lived on Fish Street, Wallingford, and was a town councillor, auctioneer and cabinet maker, aged 51 at the time of death according to a notice in *Jackson's Oxford Journal*, 19 June 1847.

BADEN HENRY BADEN-POWELL          Born 1841, Headington

Baden Henry Baden-Powell was the son of Baden Powell (born 1796). He was one of four siblings, with a further ten half-brothers and sisters arriving later (including Robert, later General Baden-Powell, famous founder of the Boy Scout movement). The 'Baden' part of the surname was adopted, it is said, in an attempt to differentiate various bits of the sprawling family; but to no avail, as everyone seems to have happily adopted the new prefix.

| | |
|---|---|
| **FUD PRATLEY** | Born 1883, Northleigh |
| **WILLIAM WATERLOO PRATLEY** | Born 1836, Witney |
| **YETTA PRAVER** | 1896–1943, Oxford |
| **GERTRUDE MINERAL PREEDY** | 1890–1977, Oxford |
| **POLLY PULLEY** | Born 1859, Wheatley |
| **BARTHOLOMEW QUELCH** | Married 1728, Oxfordshire |
| **RALPH QUELCH** | 1557–1620, Benson |

To the pious memory of Ralph Quelch, and Jane his wife,
Who slept together in bed for the space of 40 years,
Who sleep together in grave till Christ shall awaken them.
He fell asleep AD 1620 being aged 63 years
She fell asleep AD 16 …
*For the fruit of their labours they left the New Inn*
*twice rebuilt at their own charge.*
*For the fruit of their bodies they left One only son and two daughters.*
*Their son being liberally bred at the University of Oxford,*
*thought himself bound to erect this small Monument*
*Of their piety towards God*
*Of his piety towards them.*

This is from an inscription at Benson church, as noted by seventeenth-century historian Anthony Wood in *Oxfordshire Monumental Inscriptions*.

| | |
|---|---|
| **ELI MILLS RAGGETT** | 1800–1887, Woodstock |
| **ADAH SCADDING** | Born 1873, Thame |
| **DANCHERFIELD SCOTT** | Born 1858, Henley |

| | |
|---|---|
| **GOLDEN THOMAS SEATER** | Died 1851, Woodstock |
| **GLEANOR SIMENON** | Born 1893, Oxford |
| **THOSNAS SKITMORE** | Born 1840, Leigh, Witney |
| **ANSTICE SPENDELOW** | Married 1744, Oxfordshire |
| **ONO STEVENS** | Born 1780, resident of Oxford Workhouse in St Clements on the 1851 census |

*Garden robs garden!* The pathetically headlined 'Paupers robbing the Workhouse Garden' appeared in *Jackson's Oxford Journal* on 3 October 1857. Labourer William Garden and John Colley stole 'a quantity of seakale, of the value of 3s' from the garden of the Oxford Workhouse. Colley was a workhouse resident at the time. The men had no defence representing them in court, and were condemned to hard labour in prison – Garden for nine months, Colley just for one. The judgement of the prosecutor was that 'it was hardly worth putting the public to the expense of keeping him, but he would have to undergo one month's hard labour, and he gave that because he was in the company of a bad man'.

## John Fishweek Gibbs Summersell

Born 1842, Chipping Norton

## John Pudsey Welchman Sydenham

1809–1854, Hampden Manor, Kidlington

When landowners began enclosing and draining Otmoor in 1829, the farmers and agricultural labourers who had relied on the extra income generated by the wetland common's ducks and geese rebelled. At the height of these 'Otmoor Riots' in 1830, 1,000 men descended on the land to destroy enclosure fences. Local churchmen and the Conservative establishment condemned the so-called rioters, but John Pudsey Welchman Sydenham, advocate of much-needed social reform, championed the principles behind the unrest, pointing out that there were bigger issues at stake. A local rhyme protested:

> *The fault is great in Man or Woman*
> *Who steals the Goose from off a Common;*
> *But who can plead that man's excuse*
> *Who steals the Common from the Goose?*

## Mary Best Hitt Symes

Born 1875, Caversham

# TIGLATH-PILESER
Died 1848, Oxford

*Bear necessities!* Tiglath-pileser – Tig for short – is the only non-human listed in this book. He was a black bear, favourite pet of Frank Buckland (1826–1880) and his father, the eccentric Oxford University lecturer William Buckland (1784–1856). Between them they kept (and ate) a diverse menagerie of animals at their home in Christ Church College. Biographer William Tuckwell explained:

> On a certain morning in May the bear escaped from Buckland's yard, and found his way into the chapel, at the moment when a student was reading the first lesson, 2 Kings xvi, and had reached the point at which King Ahaz was on his way to meet Tiglath-pileser, King of Assyria, at Damascus. The bear made straight for the Lectern, its occupant fled to his place, and the half-uttered name on his lips was transferred to the intruder.

Tig was sometimes dressed up in university cap and gown for parties and boating trips with Buckland, and was present at an 1847 meeting of the British Association. Eventually banned from college, he retired to the Bucklands' country estate in Islip, where he learned to ride a (very brave) horse. The country idyll came to an end when Tig became a repeat offender by robbing Islip's grocer's shop and chasing sheep. Frank Buckland packed Tiglath-pileser off to London Zoo in 1847 where the bear died soon afterwards following an unsuccessful attempt to deal with his sugar-rotted teeth.

# WILLIAM BARBY THOMAS                 1810–1842, Neithrop, Banbury

# CHARLES TOMES                                    Died *c.*1840, Oxford

Oxford lawyer Charles Tomes was Secretary for the City Council, at a time when the country was in the economic doldrums as a result of the Napoleonic wars. He published declarations for the 'sub-committee for managing the Concerns of the Institution for bettering the Condition of the peaceable and industrious Poor'. As an example of their good works, on 21 January 1801 the committee met 'for the Purpose of taking into Consideration the Propriety of supplying the Poor with Corned Herrings, three Days in the Week, in Lieu of Soup; that a Sample of Herrings be laid before the Meeting.' On the 27th the resolution was 'resolved unanimously', and it was declared 'that the Society for Bettering the Condition of the Poor be invested with discretionary Power to purchase such Articles of Sustenance as shall appear to them necessary, and best calculated to answer the Purposes of the Institutions; and that they shall be at Liberty to apply the same, not only in Soup, but in any other Way that shall be thought adviseable.' Which was all a long-winded way of saying 'yes' to the corned herrings! (*Jackson's Oxford Journal*, 24 & 31 January 1801)

The Society mentioned above was providing more than 4,000 portions of soup and corned herrings per week in the early 1800s, according to an article in *Jackson's Oxford Journal* on Saturday, 4 April 1801. Tomes soldiered on – he is mentioned as failing to take up his position on the council benches in 1840 and is thought to have died later that year.

# GERALD HUGH TYRWHITT-WILSON

1883–1950,
14th Lord Berners of Farringdon House

Wilson lived in Oxford after the outbreak of the Second World War, having suffered a nervous breakdown. His book *Far From the Madding War* commemorates his Oxford years. Eccentric by choice, Tyrwhitt-Wilson kept a pet giraffe (sometimes bringing it to his tea parties), dyed all Farringdon Hall's pigeons bright colours (a tradition that exists to this day), and erected signs in his grounds including the classic 'Do not throw stones at this notice'.

# OTT WARD

Born 1876, Henley

# BLISS WARTER

Born 1850, Banbury

# GEORGE FESSEY WEBBS

Born 1791, Banbury

# ABIEL WHICHELLO

1804–1883, Tetsworth

Son of another Abiel Whichello, butcher

# HUGE JOHN WIGAN

Born 1866, Cowley

# MADRACK WILLIMAS

Born 1816, Whitchurch, Bradfield

# THERE'S NO PLACE LIKE HOME

The main roads, back lanes and copses of Oxfordshire
are a source of delight for the funny-name hunter.
From the celebrated Golden Balls Roundabout to
the subtleties of Tumbledown Hill, there is an oddity
around every corner. Of course, weird or alarming
place names can be changed, as witnessed by these
long-lost street signs from Ye Olde Oxford:

## GALLOWS BAULK
Changed to the less grim St Margaret's Lane in 1832.

## GROPECUNT LANE
The old links with prostitution were papered over when
this became Magpie Lane in the seventeenth century. It had
toyed coyly with 'Grope Lane' and 'Grove Lane' before
opting for the magpies. (Banbury had a similarly named
thoroughfare, long-since changed to Parsons Lane.)

## LONDONISSHE ROAD
Renamed Iffley Road in the nineteenth century;
perhaps, on reflection, it wasn't very much like London after all.

## MOUSECATCHER'S LANE

Became Cat Street, and is currently Catte Street, although it
isn't actually named after felines at all, but after St Catherine.

## MR KNAPP'S FREE BOARD

Don't ask (mainly because I don't know).
Became Warneford Lane in 1932.

## SLAUGHTER STREET

Known as Brewer's Lane since the eighteenth century, another
trade associated, metaphorically, with getting slaughtered.

## THE BUTTS

Archery practise – i.e. 'shooting at the butts' – had long been
out of fashion when this was renamed Cress Hill Place in 1969.

However, most daft old names linger.
After all, why change something that's guaranteed
to cheer you up every time you pass by?

My vote for the worst road names in the county goes
to neighbouring Alpha Avenue and Beta Boulevard in
Garsington. There should have been an automatic sacking
on the council committee that came up with those clangers.
No Gamma Grove or Delta Drive in Garsington … yet!

## ALLECTUS AVENUE, AMBROSDEN

This one conceals a tale of Oxfordshire's Dark Ages. Allectus was the treasurer of Carausius, a breakaway Roman-era emperor who seized power in Britain and Gaul in AD 286. Allectus, as avaricious as any other ambitious banker through the ages, murdered Carausius to become self-proclaimed emperor in AD 293, reigning for three years before dying in battle. Coins bearing Allectus' name have been found in the vicinity. Ambrosden itself was long thought to be named after Ambrosius Aurelianus, another pre-Saxon Romano-British leader who, in legend, is the grandfather of King Arthur. The town's name, however, probably means 'Ambre's hill', Ambre being an Anglo-Saxon personal name.

## ANNA PAVLOVA WAY, ABINGDON

Named after the famous ballet dancer, who lived 1881–1931. Initially with the Imperial Russian Ballet and the Ballets Russes, she later formed her own dance company and was the first ballet dancer to win international fame and tour the world. Her 'Dying Swan' is still a standard ballet cliché.

# Apple Pie Wood, Enstone

# Astral Row, Greatworth

# Backside Lane, Sibford Gower

# Badgers Close, Forest Hill

I live in Forest Hill, and when my sons were younger we used to pause on the way past Badgers Close to look for the badgers. We never did spy the elusive beast, making us wonder in what sense it can be said to be 'close'. But our local invisible badgers are not alone. There are several other nearby animals in the county, including: Bear Close, Woodstock; Cuckoo Close, Caversfield; Deers Close, Bodicote; Dog Close, Adderbury; Falcon Close, Banbury; Fox Close, Garsington, Chipping Norton and Bampton; Grebe Close and Kingfisher Close, Abingdon; Linnet Close, Burcot; Kestrel Close, Carterton; Robins Close, Barford St Michael; Salmon Close, Bloxham; and Puma Close, Benson (and that one's cheating, as it's named, like many of the Benson streets, after aircraft associated with the RAF base). There's a large area of Bicester in which the streets are all named after birds – dozens of them. A smaller aviary of roads can be found in Blackbird Leys, Oxford.

# Bean Furlong, Chacombe, Banbury

# Bears Hedge, Iffley, Oxford

# Beef Lane, Oxford

## Between Towns Lane, Chipping Norton

## Biddy's Bottom, Fulwell

## Birds Lane, Epwell

But who was the bird, and how was she slain?

## Bitterell, Eynsham

This is a private road owned by Oxford's Corpus Christi College, so you'll have to ask them what it means.

## Blewitt Court, Littlemore, Oxford

## Bliss Mill, Chipping Norton

Bliss Mill is named after William Bliss, who built a tweed mill here in 1872. He is also commemorated in the town's William Bliss Avenue. It was Bliss' need for an endless supply of mill-fuelling coal that brought the railway to the town in the 1870s. There was an early episode of Union solidarity here in 1913/14 when the millworkers went on strike for eight months. Like all Britain's mills this one was doomed, closing in 1980 and later converted into flats. The building is still a local landmark, with its dome-topped chimney intact, and the main building resembling (as Bliss intended) a stately home rather than a mill.

## Blue Boar Street, Oxford

Some medieval royal iconography has survived the ravages of the centuries. Many pubs called the Red Lion are perpetuating the memory of John of Gaunt (1340–1399), father of King Henry IV and founder of the House of Lancaster; those called the White Hart are using the icon of King Richard II (1367–1400); and the country's Blue Boars (including the one on Blue Boar Street) are making a mark on posterity for King Richard III (1452–1485) – famous these days for being unearthed under a car park in Leicester in 2012.

## Blue Row, Over Norton

BOBBY FRIAR CLOSE, COWLEY, OXFORD

BOTTOM WOOD, NR CHARLBURY

BREECHES END, CUMNOR HILL, OXFORD

BRILL ROAD, HORTON-CUM-STUDLEY

BUSH FURLONG, DIDCOT

BUTTS CLOSE, AYNHO

BUTTS LANE, MARSTON, OXFORD

BUTTS ROAD, HORSPATH; ANOTHER IN FARINGDON

BUTTS WAY, ASTON ROWANT

CAMP LANE, WARMINGTON

CATSLIP, NETTLEBED

### CECIL SHARP PLACE, HEADINGTON, OXFORD

In 1899, a group of desperado morris men from Headington Quarry
decided to earn some extra money (work at the brick works had
dried up) by busking on Christmas Eve. At Sandfield House (on the land
enclosed by modern Horwood Close, Sandfield Road and Beech Road
in Headington) they caught the ear of Cecil Sharp, folk song collector,
who was visiting friends at Sandfield. Sharp was so entranced by the
music that he invited the morris men's musician William Kimber to
return later and play the tunes for him. This not only saved the dying
tradition from extinction, it was also the beginning of the English
folk music revival, a direct link to today's hugely popular folk festivals,
including Oxfordshire's own gems at Towersey, Haddenham and, daddy
of them all, Fairport's Cropredy Convention.

## Chatterpie Lane, Combe, near Woodstock

The chatterpies are not talkative pub snacks, but magpies. In the legend of Edith Forne, who founded Osney Priory in 1129, these pies play a prominent role: as Edith was walking by the Thames, she met a rowdy flock of magpies. The birds were there on subsequent occasions, and after making enquiries of a local holy man, Edith was told that the 'chattering pies' were actually the souls of the dead in Purgatory, crying out for a religious establishment in which prayers could be said for their safe transit to Heaven. Edith, who wished to attone for past sins (she had been a mistress to King Henry I), founded the priory (which became an abbey in 1158). It was situated by the river at the back end of modern Mill Street, Oxford – the only bit remaining amongst the twenty-first-century redevelopment is the shell of the abbey's mill.

## Cleaver Square, Oxford

## Cobblers Close, Cropredy

## Cockpit Close, Woodstock

The cock pit, used for the blood sport of cock-fighting, was, indeed, close by.

## Cockshoot Close, Stonesfield

## Cockshoothill Copse, part of Wychwood Forest, near Charlbury

Another form of chicken-related sport is being commemorated here – cock-shooting. Arrows or stones were aimed at the birds in a gory early version of the fairground coconut shy. The person who killed the bird could then claim it for the oven.

## Coneygree Terrace, Chipping Norton

## CONIGREE, CHINNOR

A coneygree (or conigree) is a Norman word for a rabbit warren, conies being bunnies. It is a known 'fact' that the Normans introduced the rabbit to England after the Conquest in 1066. The Romans, however, brought the earliest specimens, breeding them for meat.

## COW POOL, BERRICK SALOME

## CREAMPOT LANE, CLOSE AND CRESCENT, CROPREDY

## CROTCH CRESCENT, MARSTON, OXFORD

## CRUMPS BUTTS, BICESTER

## CRUTCH FURLONG, BERINSFIELD

## CUCKAMUS LANE, NORTH LEIGH

Named after the village pond, filled in in 1968 and originally called Cucking Stool Pond. A cucking stool was another name for a ducking stool. This ultimate in uncomfortable seats, usually reserved for nagging wives or witches, was a chair attached to the end of a pole, which dunked the unfortunate in the water as a form of punishment.

## CUP AND SAUCER, CROPREDY

# Dairy Ground, King's Sutton

# Dead Man's Riding Wood, Fulwell

# Dead Man's Walk

This footpath runs next to the old city wall between Merton, Christ Church and Corpus Christi colleges in Oxford. It was originally the route taken by medieval Jewish funeral processions, starting at the synagogue (on the site of Christ Church's Tom Tower) and heading for the Jewish cemetery on the site of the Botanical Gardens. Ghosts, inevitably, have been sighted here many times.

# Defiant Close, Bicester

# Delly End, Hailey, near Witney

And not a delicatessen to be seen for miles … Originally a clearing for pasture in a large area of woodland, the name Delly combines valley (dell) and clearing (ley or lea). Nearby are Delly Hill and Delly Close.

# Demesne Furze, Headington, Oxford

This road marks the edge of a former area of furze (gorse) heathland. It was also the name of a character in the 1979 *Doctor Who* story *The Trail of the White Worm*.

# Divinity Road, Headington

# Doveleat, Chinnor

A leat is a watercourse associated with a watermill.

# Down End, Hook Norton

# Duck Square, Chinnor

# Eagles, Farringdon

# Fattingfield Copse, near Enstone and Heythrop

# Fiddlers Hill, Shipton-under-Wychwood

# Filley Alley, Letcombe Bassett

# First Turn, Oxford

# Flexneys Paddock, Stanton Harcourt

# Fludger Close, Wallingford

Named after benefactor Henry Fludger. Fludger's charity was set up in his will of 1817 to raise money for the elderly poor of the town.

# Forceleap Copse, Hinton-in-the-Hedges

# Friars Entry, Oxford

# Frog Lane, Milton-under-Wychwood

# Gadge Close, Thame

# Gallowstree Road, Gallowstree Common

The village of Gallowstree Common takes its name from a long-gone oak tree that was used for many centuries as a gallows. The last person was strung up here in 1825, for sheep stealing.

# Gelt Burn, Didcot

# Golden Balls Roundabout, near Nuneham Courtenay

Named after a pub, the Golden Balls, which used to stand nearby. Three golden balls are the traditional symbol of pawnbroker shops, suggesting that the pub owners had ingenious ways of enabling their skint patrons to access more cash.

# GOOSE WALK, BLOXHAM

# GOOSEY LANE, GOOSEY

# GORWELL, WATLINGTON

# GREAT BOTTOM, A COPSE NEAR ROTHERFIELD PEPPARD

# GREAT COXWELL

# GREEN HITCHINGS, GREAT MILTON

# HACKERS LANE, CHURCHILL

# HAMSTYLES, BRITWELL SALOME

# HARPSICHORD PLACE, OXFORD

# HARRY BEARS/BEAR'S BOTTOM, HEADINGTON

This is an old name for a chunk of Headington centred on the junction of Windmill Road, the Slade and Old Road. The 'Bottom' element stems from the fact that it is at the foot of Shotover Hill. Legend names Harry Bear as a local man who used to deliver messages to his friend on Lears Hill in Wheatley by shooting arrows over Shotover Hill. This is a very long journey for an arrow, which is why in other versions of the legend the projectiles are fired by a giant.

# HELL COPPICE, NEAR HORTON-CUM-STUDLEY

# HEMPLANDS, GREAT ROLLRIGHT

# HISKINS, WANTAGE

# HONEY BOTTOM LANE, DRY SANDFORD, ABINGDON

# Horse Fair, Banbury

All's fair in Banbury … Once famous for its trading fairs, the town formerly held an annual horse fair, as well as a cow fair, a leather fair, a fish fair, a cheese fair and a wool fair.

# Horsefair, Chipping Norton

# Janaway, Oxford

# Jethro Tull Gardens, Crowmarsh Gifford

Not named after the famous rock band, but after the original Tull (1674–1741), inventor of the seed drill, among other things.

# Kew Win, Didcot

# Kingston Bagpuize

This village was named after Norman looter Ralph de Bagpuis, who grabbed the land in 1066. It was called Bagpipes by American servicemen in the Second World War, and Bagpuss can never be far from your mind when you see the name on road signs.

# Logic Lane, Oxford

# Love Lane, Watlington

# Mafeking Row, Shirburn

Commemorating the Siege of Mafeking, 1899. Mafeking was where Colonel Robert Baden-Powell, founder of the Boy Scout movement, first came to fame. He was in charge of the city's defence during the Second Boer War, in a siege lasting more than 200 days.

# Meteor Close, Bicester

One of a number of roads named in honour of the nearby RAF base. Others include Spitfire Close.

# Midget Close, Abingdon

# Moody Road, Oxford

# Mosquito Lane, Benson

Not the bloodsucking insect but the aeroplane, this being RAF Benson.

# Nottingham Fee, Blewbury

This was the name of one of the three manors of the village, named after the Nottingham family who first owned the manor.

# Offal Wood, near Nettlebed

# Otters Reach, Kennington

# Oxen Piece, Great Milton

# Pack and Prime Lane, Henley-on-Thames

# Paradise Lane, Milcombe

# Paradise Street, Oxford

# Paradise Terrace, Milcombe

# Patch Ridings, Finstock

Old name for one of the tracks through Wychwood Forest.

# Peasmoor Piece

From Old English *pise* meaning 'peas', the veg in question was probably one of the wild pea plants (the Fabaceae family) that predate modern peas – possibly Marsh Trefoil (*Lotus pendunculatus*) or Birdsfoot Trefoil (*Lotus corniculatus*).

# Periwinkle Place, Blackbird Leys, Oxford

## PETHERS PIECE, BURFORD
Named after the local Pether family.

## PETTIWELL, GARSINGTON

## PICKLERS HILL, ABINGDON

## PIGGY LANE, BICESTER

## PISHILL, IN STONOR PARISH
*Taking the pishill* – for the root of these 'pise' names, see Peasmoor Piece.

## PISHILLBURY WOOD, PISHILL

## PISSEN WOOD, OFF ROCKY LANE NEAR ROTHERFIELD GREYS

## PIXEY PLACE, WOLVERCOTE, OXFORD

## POLECAT END LANE, FOREST HILL

## PUDDLEDUCK LANE, GREAT COXWELL

## PUMBRO, STONESFIELD

## PUMP LANE, THAME

## QUEEN EMMA'S DYKE, WITNEY
Or were they just good friends?

## ROGER BACON LANE, OXFORD

## ROTTEN ROW, DORCHESTER ON THAMES

## RUCK KEENE CLOSE, BICESTER
Named after a renowned local family.

## Rugge Furlong, Didcot

This one immortalises the Middle English Germainic word *rugge* meaning a ridge (or a person's or animal's back, a sense that survives in the word rucksack (i.e. 'rugge-sack')). A furlong is one eighth of a mile, judged to be the distance an ox-drawn plough team could plough before needing a rest.

## Ryegrass, Woodstock

## Saw Close (and yet so far), Chalgrove

## Sharman Beer Court, Thame

This one sounds a little less odd when you realise it's named after Adolphus Sharman Beer – see his entry in chapter 16.

## Shotover Kilns, Headington

## Skeats Bush, East Hendred

## Skimmingdish Lane, Caversfield

## Skittle Alley, Aynho

## Slaymaker Close, Headington

## Sloven Copse, near Abingdon

## Small Gains Wood, Buckland

## Spiceball Park Road, Banbury

## Spooner Close, Headington

## Squitchey Lane, Summertown, Oxford

## Tenpenny, Dorchester on Thames

# The Blowings, Freeland

# The Butts, Aynho                    (there's also one in Standlake)
Butts were targets used by archers, back in the days when you weren't allowed to leave home without a bow and a quiver of arrows.

# The Cleave, Harwell

# The Dickredge, Steeple Aston

# The Forty, Cholsey                    (the name of the village green)

# The Goggs, Watlington

# The Knob, King's Sutton

# The Lynch, East Hendred

# The Shades, Banbury

# The Slade, Headington
A name taken from a former common, enclosed in the nineteenth century. The name is from Old English *slæd*, meaning valley, specifically a flat-bottomed and damp valley. There is another Slade in Charlbury.

# The Straight Mile, Horton-cum-Studley                    (and yes, it is)

# The Tchure, Deddington
There are other Tchures in Charlton-on-Otmoor, Upper Heyford and Steeple Aston. It's a Midlands dialect name for a narrow lane.

# The Triangle, Wheatley
It's not triangular – it's named after a cafe that used to stand here.

# Threelandboard Wood, near Stoke Row

## Tinkerbush Lane, Wantage

## Titup Hall Drive, Oxford

Titup Hall was a coaching inn, on the site of the present Crown & Thistle on Old Road, Headington.

## Toot Hill Butts, Headington, Oxford

A reference to an ancient piece of land, Toot-hill Butts Furlong. 'Toot' in Old English means land on a lookout hill. 'Butt' means a strip of land next to (abutting on) a boundary, often at right angles to other ridge-and-furrow strips in a medieval field. This is not the usual sense of 'butts', however, which generally means a target used for arrow-shooting practise (see The Butts, previous).

## Tumbledown Hill, Cumnor

Turn Again Lane, Oxford

Turnagain Lane, Abingdon

Tyte End, Great Rollright

Upper Paradise, King's Sutton

Walkers Height, Finstock

Wasties Orchard, Long Hanborough

## WATER EATON ROAD, NORTH OXFORD
(this is presumably what happened after flooding)

## WEE GROVE, A COPSE NEAR IPSDEN

## WEEPING CROSS, BODICOTE

## WENRISC DRIVE, MINSTER LOVELL

## WHIRLWIND WAY, BENSON
Another one named after aeroplanes (i.e. RAF Benson).

## WILLIAM KIMBER CRESENT, HEADINGTON
Named after concertina player William Kimber, whose playing saved
English traditional dance music from oblivion. For the full story
see Cecil Sharp Place, previous. Kimber's grave can be seen in the
churchyard at Headington Quarry, complete with an engraving of his
chosen instrument.

## WINCEY VIEW, WITNEY
Not a very nice view, we assume.

## WITTENHAM CLUMPS, TWO HILLS NEAR LITTLE WITTENHAM
Also known as Mother Dunch's Buttocks, or the Berkshire Bubs
(as in boobs). Dunch was apparently Lady of the Manor at Little
Wittenham in the seventeenth century.

## WRETCHWICK WAY, BICESTER

## WROSLYN ROAD, FREELAND
Badly spelled memorial to the 'wrestling' that used to take place in
Roslyn House (originally Wrosling House).

## YE OLDE HOUSEN, EAST HANNEY

# Sources

Most of the people mentioned in *Frogley, Cockhead & Crutch* were unearthed in Oxfordshire parish and census records, along with birth, marriage and death registers. For anyone wishing to dip into the archives, the Oxfordshire History Centre in Cowley and the Westgate Library in Oxford are the best starting points.

Collecting the place names was largely a case of scouring maps and streetname directories, with http://oxford.streetmapof.co.uk giving invaluable tip-offs.

Many of the stories in the book were found in the pages of *Jackson's Oxford Journal* (1753–1928). I also took a few leads from these books:

Russell Ash's trailblazing *Potty, Fartwell & Knob* (Headline, 2007)

Montagu Burrows, *Worthies of All Souls – four centuries of English history, illustrated from the college archives* (1874)

T. Phillips (ed.), *Oxfordshire Monumental Inscriptions, from the MSS. of Antony à Wood* (1825)

Paul Sullivan, *The Little Book of Oxfordshire* (2012), *The Secret History of Oxford* (2013) and *Oxford: A Pocket Miscellany* (2011), all published by The History Press

William Tuckwell, *Reminiscences of Oxford* (1901)

The following websites were also useful:

http://archives.balliol.ox.ac.uk
www.british-history.ac.uk
www.nationalarchives.gov.uk
www.oxfordhistory.org.uk
www.oxfordtimes.co.uk
www.wikipedia.org

# About the Author

PAUL SULLIVAN lives near Oxford with his wife and two sons. A specialist in folklore with many books to his name (including *The Little Book of Oxfordshire* and *Bloody British History: Oxford*), he also researched, wrote and presented a weekly festivals and customs guide for BBC Radio 5 in the 1990s. He worked part-time in the Museum of Oxford in order to absorb the history of the area, reading widely, studying the museum's collection and visiting as many of the county's celebrated sites and events as possible. When time allows, he moonlights as a semi-professional folk singer.

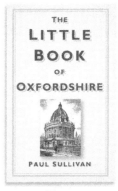

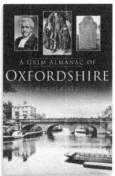

Lightning Source UK Ltd.
Milton Keynes UK
UKOW06f2340170415

249878UK00007B/71/P